"Real ideas that real-life couples can put into practice immediately—that's what I love about *Red-Hot Monogamy*! All the biblical truth and godly love life advice I've ever heard—and more—is simply and beautifully wrapped up in this one practical book. Speaking at marriage conferences about my own lost-and-found love, I've been recommending great books on sex for years. Not anymore! Bill and Pam's perspectives make *Red-Hot Monogamy* perfect for everyone—profitable for difficult, good, or even great marriages! I wish I'd had it years ago—for my own marriage enrichment and to recommend to others. And I thought my married love life sizzled *before* reading this book!"

Nancy Sebastian Meyer, national speaker
and author of *Beyond Expectations: Finding
Joy in Your Marriage*

"Bill and Pam Farrel know what it takes to make red-hot monogamy a priority. This book not only tells you why investing in your marriage is important, it tells you how to make it happen! Practical, humorous, creative, and chock-full of ideas to make your love life all it can be, *Red-Hot Monogamy* is a book all married couples need to read!"

Jill Savage, founder and executive director,
Hearts at Home, and author of *Is There
Really Sex After Kids?*

"After reading *Red-Hot Monogamy*, I was convinced and convicted that sex could be *even better!* This is a great resource to spice up your marriage and help your intimate relationship be more of what God intended. Thank you, Bill and Pam, for your encouragement NOT to settle for lukewarm. *Red-Hot Monogamy* can help any couple turn up the heat!"

Kendra Smiley, conference speaker and
author of several books, including *Be the
Parent* (Moody, January 2006).

"What a wonderful book! I could have used this over the past 20 years and will be using it in the years to come."

Steve Arterburn, bestselling author of *Every Man's Battle* and *Healing Is a Choice*

"Why settle for lukewarm lovemaking when you can have red-hot monogamy? Bill and Pam have done a great job addressing a wide range of sexual topics without making it feel like a how-to handbook. Thank you for not over spiritualizing or dancing around difficult topics. *Red-Hot Monogamy* is full or real ideas, tips, and suggestions to make married sex fun, regardless of what phase of life you may be facing."

Marita Littauer, president, CLASServices Inc., speaker, and author of *The Praying Wives Club* and *Love Extravagantly*

MONOGAMY

BILL & PAM FARREL

HARVEST HOUSE PUBLISHERS

EUGENE, OREGON

Cover photo © davies and starr / Stone / Getty Images

Cover by Left Coast Design, Portland, Oregon

Published in association with the literary agency of Alive Communications, Inc., 7680 Goddard Street, Suite 200, Colorado Springs, CO 80920.

RED-HOT MONOGAMY
Copyright © 2006 by Bill and Pam Farrel
Published by Harvest House Publishers
Eugene, Oregon 97402
www.harvesthousepublishers.com

Library of Congress Cataloging-in-Publication Data

Farrel, Bill, 1959–
  Red-hot monogamy / Bill and Pam Farrel.
    p. cm.
  Includes bibliographical references.
  ISBN-13: 978-0-7369-1608-0 (pbk.)

  1. Sex in marriage—Religious aspects—Christianity.   2. Spouses—Religious life.   I. Farrel, Pam, 1959–   II. Title.
  BV4596.M3.F375 2006
  248.8'44—dc22

                                                              2005026892

Printed in the United States of America

14   15   / VP-CF /   15   14   13

To Pam

*M*y angel, my lover, and my best friend,
You have taken me to heights I never knew existed,
You helped me see possibilities
I never dreamed I'd see.

*T*hank you for making red-hot monogamy
an incredible journey!

Bill

To Bill

*W*e've had 25 years of red-hot monogamy…
how about at least 25 more?

*Y*our love has given me wings to soar.

*Y*ou have been my "mirror," and I am forever grateful.

*Y*our angel,

Pam

*W*e love because God first loved us.

1 JOHN 4:19 GNT

CONTENTS

I

Sex! What Makes It Red-Hot?

How to Create Some Steamed Heat!

On a cold, clear January night, the stars flickered in the sky like individual candles calling lovers into one another's arms. Inside, the lights were romantically dim. Music softly serenaded lovers as they reminisced over 25 years of memories.

Anita Renfroe then stepped to the podium in the ballroom and announced, "We are here tonight to celebrate the righteous red-hot monogamy of Bill and Pam Farrel." The crowd laughed as we looked at each other in shocked amusement.

While we were recovering from her statement, our oldest son, Brock, stepped to the podium to say grace at the Twenty-fifth

Anniversary Dinner Gala we were sharing with 300 of our closest friends. He introduced himself by saying, "Hi, everyone. I am Brock Farrel, the first product of my parents' righteous red-hot monogamy."

At that moment the concept for this book was conceived. It was embarrassingly awesome to have our love referred to as red-hot monogamy. In our hearts we know this is the dream of every married couple. We were created as sexual beings with an incredible capacity for pleasurable experiences. We were created with an intense desire to be connected to another human. We were also created with incredible emotional potential. As a result, sex can be the greatest source of pleasure on earth or it can be the greatest source of disappointment and insecurity. *Red-Hot Monogamy* is our attempt to help you develop a love life you will love.

Is It Really That Red-Hot?

You may wonder why we chose to write *this* book. What would possess a couple to boldly take on such a personal topic as marital sex? Well, it really chose us. We have been teaching on relationships since we were newlyweds. Our first published book, *Pure Pleasure: Making Your Marriage a Great Affair,* was coauthored with Jim and Sally Conway. It was motivated by the chaos and fallout of the sexual revolution. We wondered how people could be so inundated with sex in the culture, on TV, in magazines, and on the Internet, and yet be so dissatisfied and hurting in their own private sex lives. The main point, we emphasized, was that sex is *not an event—sex is a relationship.* In *Red-Hot Monogamy,* we pick up the conversation and will give you practical, personal tips for creating the kind of sex life that really works.

We have a lot of fun with the topic, but we actually think sex is a serious matter. So many lives can either be destroyed or enhanced by the way sex is used. It is a lot like atomic energy. Plutonium can be used to produce abundant energy or to enhance medical science. In less scrupulous hands, that same plutonium can be detonated in a bomb that destroys everything in its wake.

Yes, sex is powerful, and, as with everything beautiful that God created, Satan tries to steal, distort, and misuse sex as a weapon against the heart of man. Take music. It has stirred the hearts of every generation of men and women. It can inspire confidence, lower stress, and set incredibly romantic moods. Yet look at musicians such as Curt Cobain and Janis Joplin, who died from misusing drugs in some melodic, tragic lostness.

Or how about medical research that has discovered the cure for polio and made possible things such as limb replacement surgery and organ transplants? These are all great things, yet that same scientific field created the means for the destruction of human life in abortion. Dancing is another example. Dance form, like ballet, is a beautiful art. However, dance can be distorted and misused, as it is in strip clubs around the world. Sex is the same. It is a gift to be valued and protected so it cannot be used as a weapon.

We must make a choice regarding sexual expression. We will either utilize it as a deviant, destructive power or we will harness its potential to keep love alive and vibrant in our marriage relationships.

In a marriage, sex is the spice that rescues our relationships from becoming mundane pursuits of chores. Adult life is filled with responsibilities. We have mortgages to pay, yard work to maintain, laundry to clean, cars to service, and so on. But none of us got married so we could load up on chores. We got married out of hope. We got married because we believed there was some kind of magic between us. We got married because we believed we could have great sex together. A satisfying sex life can add dignity to all the other pursuits of life. It is the thing to look forward to after a dull or miserable day at work. Sex is the moment of connection that creates a deep bond, even when sprinkled weeks or months apart. Sexual union adds an underlying deposit of strength that can help hold couples together when life threatens to pull them apart.

Though sex is undeniably an important aspect of a healthy marriage, it is challenging to keep sex in its proper place. Ask any married couple. If they are honest, they will share that the act of marital sex is at the same time a great source of delight, an agonizing source of frustration, an intimate place of together-ness, and an awkward place of embarrassment or trauma. The topic of sex, by its very nature, elicits an emotional response. You will rarely get a ho-hum response when you ask someone about their sex life. Sexual intimacy, by its very nature, was designed by the Creator as a gift for the soul. At times people will try to tell us that sex is not a big deal, but that is usually an attempt to hide their frustration over not developing the intimacy they had hoped for.

It still amazes me (Bill) that, after 25 years of being together, sex still has such an effect on Pam and me. When we are in sync with each other and enjoying each other often, life is good. The sky is bluer, the sun is brighter, and all tasks seem easier. I know I am easily distracted by Pam when we are in tune with each other, but I accomplish more in the other areas of my life. I think more clearly and have more emotional energy to invest in my goals. My life stops when I get a peek at her breasts. I freeze in my tracks when she winks at me and gives me that "Do you wanna?" look. It takes time out of my schedule, but I still get more done. I will never understand that.

It also amazes me how ridiculous I can be when we are not as sexually active as I would like. I become sad, frustrated, and even angry. I snap at dumb things in life and become unproduc-tive. Everything seems harder and less interesting. I find myself thinking weird thoughts, such as: *I thought she cared about me. She used to think I was attractive. Why is everything else in life more important than me?* To be sure, these are overreactions, but I don't seem to have any defenses against thinking this way, except, of course, reengaging sexually with Pam.

Because we recognize the powerful impact of good marital sex, our goal is to fan the flame of your love. God gave you this gift to be enjoyed, savored, and strengthened. When you enhance your overall marital well-being, the rest of your life is more effective in accomplishing God's purpose for you.

DO NOT DISTURB

We have a vivid example of our kids knowing that our love life is alive and well. Our oldest son, Brock, was dating Hannah, who is now his wife. All four of us parents are involved with Christian publishing. Hannah's folks own a Christian bookstore, and we write some of the books that go in it. So when Hannah and Brock's relationship started to get serious, we decided to converge in Atlanta for the Christian booksellers convention. We asked the kids to come down from Liberty University, where they were attending summer school, and meet us in Atlanta. On our first day there, Bill went to a business meeting while I got ready for an evening appointment. To avoid an embarrassing intrusion during my shower, I hung the "Do Not Disturb" sign on the door. Brock was with Hannah's family and planning to meet us for dinner. While he was walking to our hotel, a sudden thunderstorm hit that completely drenched him. Brock's soggy clothes were dripping on the carpet as he entered the hotel. He was desperate to get into our room and change, but when he arrived at the door he noticed the "Do Not Disturb" sign barricading his entrance. From the hallway outside our room, I heard a loud exclamation,

"Oh, man, I can't believe this! Do not disturb! I know what that means. Why now? It's the middle of the afternoon!"

I laughed as I opened the door. Brock seemed very relieved that it was only me, and that I was fully clothed.

"Whew! Thanks, Mom. I saw the sign and I thought, 'I can't interrupt Mom and Dad having sex!' That is just TMI!" (Too much information.)

"It's okay, honey. Dad isn't even here. But it's amazing and awesome that the first thought in your 20-year-old mind is that you'd be interrupting our love life!"

"Yeah, it's weird. I don't really like to think about you and Dad that way, but I know I want a marriage just like yours when I've been married 25 years too."

RED HOTS

In junior high, my (Pam's) favorite candies were red hots or Hot Tamales. That zesty cinnamon flavor really made me feel alive. I think that is why so many euphemisms for sex are related to "red," "hot," or "fire." Think about it. "Come on, baby, light my fire," "Hunka hunka burnin' love," Jerry Lee Lewis' "Great Balls of Fire," or the pounding back beat of the '70s dance hit, "Fire!"

We whisper things in the throes of passion, such as "You set my heart ablaze" or "I am consumed by your love." We use word pictures that describe sex as being much like a forest fire consuming whatever is in its path. We long to be in a love relationship that feels as powerful as a raging fire. During the San Diego fires, the blaze was so strong that in one section it jumped a ten-lane freeway. Don't we all long to be loved so intensely that nothing can stop or quench our lover's burning passion?

Why do we long for intense, all-consuming love? Because God designed us to give and receive love that way. Our physical form and our desire to make ready use of it are no surprise to God. We are hardwired for passion. Once Bill and I were meeting with a well-known psychologist. He had a stack of research on his desk about the functioning of the central nervous system. He shared his fascination with us at his new discovery. He explained that the neurological path we use when we sing praise to God or pray is the same path traveled when we engage in sexual intimacy. It certainly seems a person who is passionate about God has a head start on passion in a marriage because the path is well used from head to heart.

Other studies back this up. Couples that attend church rate their sex life with the highest possible rating. Couples that pray together daily also give their sex life five stars. (There's new motivation to pray!) Couples that are in a small group or a friendship circle that believes in long-term love tend to have long-term, sexually satisfying relationships. And couples that are in long-term, married, monogamous relationships rate their overall sexual satisfaction much higher than their single counterparts. So, a statistically accurate portrayal of sex in the city would tell the stories of the love lives of the pastor and his wife or of other couples sitting in the pews each Sunday. That's where the sizzling sex really is—in the marriages of those who are passionately committed to God and each other. Those are some headlines you don't see everyday.

MONOGAMOUS HEADLINES

Think about it. What if some of our commercials and slogans were rewritten to more accurately describe how to find sex that sizzles?

Got Sex? No? Then go to Sunday school.

Non-Desperate Housewives. This week's episode depicts the happily married, sexually satisfied lives of three female Bible study facilitators and their faithful husbands.

97110, (*not* 90210, the zip code of Hollywood, but rather the zip code of Cannon Beach Conference Center, a place that offers outstanding Christian couples' conferences on the romantic Oregon Coast).

And nix Howard Stern. If a TV show really wanted to capture true, fulfilling, romantic love portraying red-hot monogamy, they should send the cameras to some of the United Marriage Encounter or Lifeway's Celebrate Marriage weekends. Those are the places in which couples who are sweetly, amazingly, and passionately in love with each other show up.

So move over, Hugh Hefner, with your counterfeit sexual exploits. The real deal is found behind closed doors in the lives of our seminary students, everyday believers, professors, pastors, and missionaries. (It is interesting that the most common sexual position is called "missionary" position.) Passion, the intense sexuality that is pure, fulfilling, and powerful, would be more likely found in the bedroom of a couple who said "I do" at the altar, not a couple living together or experiencing a one-night stand. What the media portrays and what is reality are two very different things. The truth is that 90 percent of couples living together describe their relationship as "on the rocks." And couples who cohabitate, if they ever do make it to the altar, are twice as likely to divorce as couples who did not live together.[1]

We don't point this out to make you feel shame or guilt if you made that cohabitation choice. Instead, we want to let you in on the truth that people who are married have the hottest sex lives. So we've now let the cat out of the bag: Studies all indicate the best sex happens in a long-term, monogamous, committed marriage relationship. The best sex is not found in Las Vegas or on some porn screen. No, the best of what sex is, the most wonderful examples of true fulfilling and passionate sexuality, is found inside the private bedroom walls of committed married couples.

The media is filled with all kinds of pictures of sexuality, but they are lies and misrepresentations of the real thing. Move over, Victoria! Sizzling sex was God's secret long before you got ahold of it! Do you think the world needs more real-life examples of righteous red-hot monogamy? Want to join the club of couples who have a long-term, happy marriage with a deeply satisfying and fulfilling sex life? Then you've come to the right place.

The world needs to see more couples who have strong marriages. One component to strong, influential love is a satisfying sex life. People will be able to tell that you two have red-hot monogamy. You won't have to say a word! They will see it in the sparkle of your eyes, in the smile on your face, and in the skip in your step. People will catch on that you and your mate are madly in love from the way you hold hands or touch as you pass one another in the hallway. When sparks are flying, no one has to say a word. Everyone can tell when someone is in love.

INFLUENTIAL LOVE

Wouldn't you love to be the poster couple for the real thing? You are reading this book because you long for all the wonderful benefits that accompany a fulfilling sex life. Read on, and you will gain the skills and principles to have a lifetime of red-hot monogamy. You will become the role model for all that is right and good in love and marriage.

Bill and I have role models too. At one of our conferences we met a couple who were both in their eighties. During the break the wife came up and whispered a question. "Pam, you've been talking about having a God-filled life that leads to passion. Is there a Guinness world record for how many times a couple over 80 has had sex in one year? Because I think my husband and I have broken it."

I answered, "I don't know if there is a record, but I do know I want to be you when I grow up!"

CAUTION: RED-HOT MONOGOMY

We are aware that people have different comfort levels with discussions about sexuality. Some of us are children of the '60s and '70s and are quite open about sex. One thing the free love movement accomplished was moving the discussion of sex to the public arena. You may have been one of those militants who painted a flower on your cheek and donned a peasant blouse and skirt and marched with a sign that read "Make love, not war." You feel you have been freed up from oppressive Victorian views of sexuality and are uninhibited in expressing your views. (We do think that the '60s gave people freedom in this area of discussing sex, but that same freedom, in the general population, wasn't handled very well. The so called "free love" ended up costing us a lot more than we ever bargained for.) Nonetheless, some of us have sat in classes on human sexuality or at least read a book or two on the topic. We may have even pulled the *Kama Sutra* off the shelf in a bookstore when we thought no one would be looking.

However, others prefer to keep the lights off and their mouths shut when it comes to the area of sexuality. The children of these couples may wonder how they ever got here because Mom and Dad never talk about sex. A few of us try our best, on occasion, to talk to our kids about the birds and bees, but euphemisms and word pictures can sometimes lead to miscommunication and confusion.

Like the three-year-old who went with his dad to see a litter of kittens. On returning home, he breathlessly informed his mother that there were two boy kittens and two girl kittens. "How did you know?" his mom asked. "Daddy picked them up and looked underneath," he replied. "I think it's printed on the bottom."

THE CREATOR'S HEART

We will try our best to balance God's holy reverence of the gift of sex with God's cosmic sense of humor about the topic. Really, think about it. Think about the plumbing and the actual act of sex. God came up with the whole system. One that requires great energy and unique positioning and usually happens when we are completely naked. He could have made it so that we propagated the species by cutting off a finger and placing it in a jar of water like a rhododendron plant. But God didn't do that. We think He may have smiled and winked when He created sex. We will seek to discuss the very serious, and the amazingly personal, topic of sex with respect for the gift. However, to make the journey a bit less like seventh-grade health class and more like a romantic honeymoon night, we will add in a dash of humor, and we pray, a whole lot of practical ideas to fan the flame of your love life.

If for any reason you are offended by something we say, just take a felt-tip marker and cross it out. This is your book. This is your love life. This is a private journey to the heart of your spouse (with a few stops at places like the erogenous zone and G-spot). Personalize the principles. Morph the map. Edit the instructions. Your sex life is like clay. In creating a super sex life, there are three sets of hands molding the art: yours, your mate's, and the Creator's. Think of us as simply the potter's wheel. We'll keep the topic spinning while you and your spouse and God create a masterpiece of love.

But please don't blame us if our discussion is candid and honest. We take our example from God. He wrote an entire book dedicated to marital love and sexuality—the Song of Songs (or Song of Solomon, as it is often entitled). We will be referring back to the couple God uses in this book of the Bible as our couple of reference. We figured, because they are dead, they won't mind us talking about their private lives. And since God first published their story, the Song of Songs seems a safe place to stimulate our discussion.

Ken and Barbie

When I (Pam) was a little girl, my sister and I played with Barbies for hours under the shade of the lilac bush or in our downstairs bedroom. We had lots of girl Barbies, but even back then good men were in short supply. We'd borrow our brother's Johnny West, Cartwright action figures, and G.I. Joes. We usually argued over who got to date "Little Joe." What we asked for Christmas every year, and never received, was a Ken doll. If we could just get our hands on this hunk of a man, we'd have someone appropriate for Barbie to date. Ken sure seemed like Mr. Right.

Unlike our unfortunate Barbies, the young bride in Song of Songs did hook Mr. Right, or shall I say, Mr. More than Right! Her Mr. Right was the king of all Israel! And the sweet, humble Shulamite woman was in awe that God brought their lives together. There are few things better in life than feeling this way about your husband or wife. We all want to believe our spouses are miraculous gifts of God, but marrying the right person does not happen by accident.

We'll be checking in on this couple from time to time, noting the strengths and weaknesses of their intimate life. This was Solomon's first love, and he made wise, right choices in this relationship. Later on, he must have experienced a midlife crisis because he began to make unwise decisions. He is a great example of our modern world. He started well, as well as anyone has ever started. He was enamored with his wife, and they were in sync socially, spiritually, emotionally, and physically. But then he got distracted. He started believing there was something better than a committed, monogamous relationship. He gave his heart away to other women and other pursuits. It wasn't long before his energy was spent and he could no longer live by the wisdom he had dispensed to so many others. (That's what happens when you break God's rules of love. Sex is like a loaded pistol. It can shoot down the enemies of love, such as lack of time, fear, and loneliness, but too often sex is misused and then it's like shooting yourself in the foot—it hurts.)

Let's give this biblical couple some more modern nicknames, and shall we also set aside all the royal titles? (We don't know about you, but none of our best friends are His Royal Highness or Duchess or Duke of anything.) So we'll simply call King Solomon, Sol, and for the Shulamite woman, let's call her Sunny. Sol and Sunny will become our case study couple.

THE BIG PICTURE

Recently, our van quit in the middle of the road. I (Pam) had to call AAA to come rescue me. While I was waiting, I pulled out our trusty owner's manual so I would have a clue of what might be going on with my vehicle. I have found this manual to be an informative book detailing how the car is *supposed* to run.

In the same way, when we first got our computer years ago, I had Bill buy me *PC for Dummies* or some other book with a similar title because someone had to know more about this box sitting on this desk than I did. Although things felt awkward at first and I had to consult the manual often, after a while I got the hang of using my computer. The principles of the book have become quite normal and natural for me now. We all depend on manuals for information for various things. Or we can go to a search engine on the Internet and find helpful information regarding almost any fix we find ourselves in. Well, the Song of Songs is a kind of manual on how to fan the flame of love. Sol and Sunny will be the characters in the human drama of life to show us what things are turn ons and what are turn offs in this journey to sexual fulfillment.

WHY HAVE SEX?

Okay, we know some of you are laughing and saying, "You've got to be kidding! Why did they ask that question? The answer is obvious—it feels great!" Well, yes, we are aware of that. And we hope you are one of the fortunate couples who is experiencing great sex. This book will be packed with ideas on how to enhance your sex life and perhaps increase the frequency so you can experience that ecstasy more often. However, for a moment, push "pause" on the pleasure button while we look at all the reasons why God invented this thing called sex.

Procreation. This one is a bit obvious. Sex creates babies. For the human race to go forward, sex has to take place. Social studies show it is preferable for the children if they are born into a loving family with both a mom and a dad united in marriage.

Proclamation. When a couple marries, their act of consummation is a symbolic picture of the wedding of Christ and His church. In a real sense, each time a couple enjoys each other sexually, it is a proclamation to Satan that God's plan of love will win out over Satan's misguided attempt to dethrone the Lord in the Garden of Eden. A happily married couple, one united emotionally, spiritually, and sexually, is one of the best antidotes to the evil in the world because love is proclaimed.

Reconnection. Life is busy, and that is no surprise to God, so He planned a yearning to be together into the human soul. The deep intellectual, emotional, and spiritual connection that happens during sex is progressive. Good sex makes us yearn for more good sex, so a wonderful cycle of marital union can develop that will keep a couple coming back together over and over again.

Recreation. God actually thinks sex should be fun. In the Old Testament, when a king spotted Isaac and Rebekah caressing in a private moment, the word he used to describe their activity is "sporting with" (Genesis 26:8). That sounds a whole lot like fun to us. In addition, if you do a quick read through the Song of Songs, you see that the king and his newlywed wife are enjoying their relationship immensely. They even have code words for sex and sexual acts. They play games to build their anticipation of being together, and later in the book, we'll see just how much this couple enjoyed their sexual relationship. Song of Songs is all about a couple who enjoys a healthy sexual life, and God included it in the canon of Holy Scripture to remind us that that sex is supposed to be enjoyable.

Rejuvenation. Sex within the context of marriage is good for your emotional and physical well-being. Sex raises your endorphin level, so it makes you happier. Sex even burns calories.

> According to the calorie counter on the Health Status website, an hour of sex burns 250 calories, the same amount as an hour of walking. To better put this number in perspective, sixty minutes of sleeping burns 55 calories, and an hour of running burns 800. Assuming that one did not make any alterations in his or her diet, by engaging in an hour of sex every day, one would lose a pound every two weeks.[2]

> Kissing burns calories, too. Professor Bryant Stamford, PhD of the University of Louisville, postulates that a deep, passionate kiss may double your basic metabolic rate and burn as many as two calories a minute. Do the math. Kissing for 15 minutes burns approximately 30 calories. If one were to kiss passionately for

15 minutes, that might lead to other calorie burning activities…[3]

Of course, sex does not qualify as the cornerstone of your aerobic workout program, but it is a great addition. We like what Janet Lee of Gymamerica.com has to say about how many calories are burned during sex:

> Let's put it this way: If you're planning to make sex a part of an already active lifestyle, great. But if you're relying on it to lose weight or tone up, you'd need to spend hours a day in the sack. According to the energy expenditure tables compiled by exercise physiologists and found in the *Health and Fitness Instructors Handbook* (Human Kinetics, 1997), sex burns anywhere from 60 to 120 (the lower range for foreplay and the upper range for particularly vigorous sex) calories an hour for a 130-lb. woman and 77 to 155 calories an hour for a 170-lb. man. Considering that running burns around 600 calories an hour, you can see that sex is not the most efficient mode of weight loss. In fact, foreplay takes about the same amount of energy as sitting around on the couch, and a more rousing session that might wake up the neighbors is still only the equivalent of a slow walk. But really, who's counting?[4]

PRACTICE MAKES PERFECT

For some of you, the subtitle *Making Your Marriage Sizzle* has you salivating in anticipation. You are excited that you will have a little more sex over the next few weeks. You can't wait to put this book down and whisk your spouse into the bedroom for your "hands-on homework" lessons.

For others of you, the subtitle strikes terror in your soul. Sex to you has not been "all that." Perhaps you have been the victim of sex used out of context (rape, molestation, or even rushed pre-marital sex in the back of a pickup). These memories leave you cold, disinterested, afraid, or numb to the whole idea of sex—even sex with your marriage partner. We will attempt to move everyone forward, no matter where you are on this continuum. For some of you, this book will be the key to unlock the hurt and put you on the road to healing by connecting you with resources for future growth and help in this vital area. For you, we pray our words and resources will be like going to the dentist. It isn't much fun when you look at the appointment on the calendar, but the guy can make your smile brighter and your self-confidence grow if you give him a chance. We are not saying this to make light of some really hard, extremely painful situation you have experienced. Rather, we are holding out God's power to give you the hope and help you need to reclaim the gift He designed for *you*, a gift He created to bless *you*, to encourage *you*, to fulfill *you*. Contrary to what you may have felt or experienced in the past, God had *you* in mind when He designed the gift of sex. Satan tried to steal the gift from you; God wants to give you the gift of enjoyable sex back again. Because of this, we have prayed that every person who has any emotional pain at all connected to sex will discover a healing balm of hope and the path to wellness within the pages of this book.

Others of you love the gift and, like on Christmas morning, you can't wait to unwrap it. You have experienced just enough fulfillment and just enough satisfaction that you are wanting more of the same great feeling you have known in precious moments of connection. You have experienced the deep enrichment that happens on every level: emotionally, physically, and spiritually, and you long for more of those experiences with the one whom your "soul loves" (Song of Songs 3:4 NASB).

You have desires to be like a passionate painter, and you want to sketch a masterpiece of love with your mate. You are like a master chef who longs to please the palate of his patrons, in this case your spouse. You want to be the well-trained Olympic athlete who excels to gain the victory, and in this scenario, the victory is a lifelong pursuit of passion that is both enriching and fulfilling. You are a conductor, and you long to create a symphony of love. But just like the painter, the chef, the athlete, and the conductor, perfection doesn't happen in just a few weeks. However, like all those who are experts in their fields of endeavor, you start someplace. This is that someplace. It is *Red-Hot Monogamy 101: An Introduction to the Principles and Practices of Fanning the Flame of Love.*

All we ask is that you, as a couple, set aside the next few weeks to learn (and—praise God—practice!) what is on the pages of this book. Still, some of you might be asking, "What if I am the only one in the marriage who wants to work on our love life?" We can work with that. Anyone who learns to love better, anyone who makes their mate a priority is bound to see some improvement in the overall status of his or her marriage. After all, what spouse can resist being loved unconditionally and with enthusiasm?

Hands-on Homework

At the end of every chapter we will offer some "practice drills" (more people would go to college if classes offered these kind of homework assignments). So let's start with our first "hands-on assignment." Select one of the two options below and begin fanning the flame of your love life today:

1. Right now, with your marriage partner, weave your fingers together and pray a simple prayer entrusting your love life to God. Even a short sentence that invites Him to be a part of the adventure ahead will be fine. So perhaps something such as: *God, thank You for my spouse. What a gift he or she is to my life. Please fan the flame of our love as we read this book together. Meet us and give us the good gifts You have planned and promised to us. Amen.*

2. If you are reading this as a solo venture, then right now, or as you go to bed tonight, go to your spouse or snuggle up next to him or her, and place your arms around him or her and simply pray. (Praying aloud is best, but silently will also do): *God, thank You for the gift of (your spouse's name). I am so thankful You brought him or her into my life as a gift. Place Your good hand of love on our life, Lord. Amen.*

Red-Hot
ROMANCE IDEAS

1. Send a gift in the mail that draws your spouse's heart home to you. You probably won't even have to enclose a note if you send her a nightie, some provocative panties, or something sexy for him to wear.

2. If you hear "your song" on the radio, simply call his or her cell phone and hold your phone up to the speaker and let the song do the romancing.

3. Send a handmade card. Most computers now have programs to personalize a message. One Valentine's Day, Bill inserted pictures of the front covers of all of our books onto separate greeting cards. He then created a twist of words that celebrated our love. For example, "It's been a Pure Pleasure being married to you." And, "If Men Are Like Waffles and Women Are Like Spaghetti, my pantry is filled with your love."

4. Send a unique gift box in the mail: a treasure chest with an invitation to "unlock my passion," a love note buried under a layer of dried rose petals, a scroll on antique-looking paper inviting your mate out for a fancy night on the town. (For a big bang, insert the rolled-up scroll through a beautiful, brand-new ring in your lover's size.)

5. Picture this!

    - Send a photo e-mail invitation (this picture should only contain what you'd be willing to have go out on the Internet worldwide, just to be on the safe side).

- Create a photo postcard of the two of you and on the back, write a thank-you for a special memory and an invitation out to another romantic activity.

- Make a photo slide show with many pictures of the two of you. Set it to your favorite song and e-mail the show to your loved one.

- Have a "glamour shot" taken and slip the picture on his or her desk with a provocative note or card on the back.

- Create a photo collage for his or her office.

6. Leave a heart made of Play-Doh or clay on his or her desk or nightstand and insert a card with an invitation for some red-hot monogamy that night sticking out of the heart.

7. Write your invitations for sex in the steam on the bathroom mirror as your lover takes his or her shower.

8. Sit facing each other as if you are looking in the mirror, touching fingertips, and then one of you takes the lead. While you maintain physical contact, your partner moves in unison with you.

9. Re-create your first date. If you can still fit into them, wear the same clothes. If not, at least go to the same places.

10. Go back to the place you first said "I love you" and say "I love you" again.

11. Go on a date to the place you got engaged and share memories of the happiest days you have experienced since then.

12. Go back to the location you honeymooned and have a second honeymoon.

13. Read a piece of classical romantic literature together: *Sense and Sensibility, Jane Eyre, Romeo and Juliet.*

14. Check out a book from the library or buy a book of love poems. Sit in front of the fireplace in each other's arms and take turns reading poems to each other.

15. Write a love song. Even if you can't sing it, you can read the lyrics.

16. Write your own love poem. Even a simple "Roses are red…" rendition will make him or her smile.

17. Rewrite a love song that is popular and personalize the lyrics to your relationship. (A "Weird Al" Yankovic or Anita Renfroe parody that makes your lover laugh is a unique twist to this idea.) You can also reword the tune to send a more serious invitation or message.

18. Is there a line from a song that you can hum into your lover's ear as he or she falls to sleep at night that will fan the flame of love? This can also work to encourage your spouse in a tense public setting or when he or she is under stress. It can remind your lover that there is more to life than work and that red-hot monogamy can make things feel better.

19. Buy a box of chocolate. Take a few of the chocolates out, and in the paper cups place a few other trinkets and gifts: jewelry, a key, a tiny love note, tickets to a play or movie, a flower, etc.

20. Create a romance almanac. Create lists of: Places We Have Loved to Go, Restaurants We Love to Eat At, Sexual Positions We Have Tried, Positions Yet to Try, 10 Best Things About You, 20 Romantic Movies Still to See, 10 Books on Marriage Still to Read, Dream-Date List, Places We Want to Vacation, Concert Schedules, Drama Options, etc.

21. Take a calendar (you can often pick up a free one at Hall-mark stores) and write in important dates (anniversaries, birthdays, possible date ideas). Or write in something you love about your spouse each Monday, someplace you want to meet him or her each Tuesday, etc. Write in unique an-niversaries: the anniversary of the day of your first date, the first "I love you," the first kiss, the day you met, etc. Give the calendar to your spouse not as a list of expecta-tions, but as a list of invitations. Let him or her respond to each invitation.

22. Make a romantic Rolodex. Give him or her the info to succeed with you romantically. Make Rolodex cards for florists, clothing stores, restaurants, hobby stores, Internet sites you have bookmarked, etc.

23. Create a series of thank-you notes. Send one a day for as many days as you can think of something to thank your mate for. Some things to be thankful for are: his or her character, things he or she has done for you, his or her commitment to you. One line on a card day after day will make a big impact.

24. Make his or her favorite meal. Add a white linen table-cloth, candlelight, flowers, and music. You might even wear a provocative waiter or waitress outfit—then ask for your tip with a wink and a smile.

25. Have an old-fashioned evening. Send a formal invitation, come to the door with flowers and chocolates, open doors for her, and perhaps find a malt shop or some other nos-talgic place to go on the date. Find a Lover's Lane where you can park, "look at the moon," and steam up the car windows a bit. Give her a kiss under the light at the door at the end of the evening.

2

Bringing the Honeymoon Home

MAKING SEX A PRIORITY

ime, or lack of it, is the biggest enemy of intimacy. Half of all Americans say they are too busy, and two-thirds say stress is negatively affecting their lives.[1] Dave and Claudia Arp, authors of *No Time for Sex*, were conversing with one of their psychologist friends who said, "If you don't talk, think, or read about sex, you'll soon forget about it!"[2] Cliff and Joyce Penner, for their book *The Gift of Sex*, interviewed several thousand people, and 75 percent said that lack of time was the greatest frustration in their sex life.[3] After signing the contract for this book, we sat down with our calendars and marked off the months we thought we'd need to write it. Then life changed.

Bill went from full-time freelancing to a full-time pastoral position at a church while also keeping our writing and speaking commitments—in essence, he has two nearly full-time careers. In that change came a two-hour round-trip commute for Bill and our son Caleb. Then God blessed us with more speaking opportunities and my schedule picked up. Then another happy event took place: Our oldest son proposed to his girlfriend and they set a date, and then he and his fiancée decided that date was just too far away so they moved it up. We are thrilled with our new daughter-in-law, so of course we wanted to be very involved in wedding plans and celebrations. After five months of commuting we grew tired of it, so we fixed up our home and put it on the market—and it sold in five days! Then we frantically had to figure out where to move just a few weeks before the wedding. In addition to this, we had two books due in this time frame along with our regular parenting responsibilities and speaking schedule. If any couple could claim no time for sex, we'd be in the running. Yet in all of this we have amazingly been able to keep the home fires burning. How? We chose to make sex a priority.

When scheduling demands first began appearing, we happened to be in the car driving to some obligation and began to talk over the situation. At first I (Pam) was a little frustrated and a bit melodramatic.

"Bill, I am going to call the publisher and tell them I can't write a book about sex if I am not going to have any while I write it!"

"Pam," my husband replied calmly, "I can see why you might feel that way. We have and always will be authentic in our writing. I don't know about you, but I'd like to try to fan the flame of our love life instead of bailing on the project."

"You know, Bill, this is where many couples are at. No time for sex. I was watching some talk show in my hotel room last week, and the host was saying that most Americans should cut their commitments in half if they wanted to get a sex life back again."

"I am sure many couples need to take a hatchet to their calendar, Pam, but we've always been a busy couple and yet made time for sex."

"True. But this time it seems more difficult."

"It can't be impossible, though. God wouldn't call us to an impossible schedule that would starve our sex life."

"Okay, Bill, here's the deal. Before when things got crazy, we'd call a time-out and head to a hotel for 48 hours and have a private marriage conference. Just order room service and have sex and relax. What if we tweak that idea?"

"I'm listening…"

"What if we make this an eight-week book? You know, an eight-week fan-the-flame refresher course? But I think we need to test the idea ourselves for eight weeks and *then* write it."

"Sounds like a great idea, honey!" Bill reached over and put his hand under my skirt, "When do we start?" he asked, smiling.

"Right now if you want, but you'll have to pull over and get us a room. Seriously, let's make a concerted effort to make sex a priority during the next eight weeks and see if it heats things up a bit despite the schedule and responsibilities we are carrying."

Then we began to discuss how to bring the honeymoon home again.

EIGHT WEEKS TO FAN THE FLAME

Think about it. In the next three months do you have eight weeks you two can set aside to make sex a priority? You don't have to quit your job or spend a month in Europe or two weeks in Hawaii (although that might be great). You just need eight weeks where you both can say, "You are my priority." If you are taking the nursing state boards or the bar exam, start the eight weeks after the test, but other than some extremely demanding responsibility, set aside the next two months for some red-hot monogamy. (Remember all the stuff we are responsible for? We did it and kept our day jobs. So can you.)

We found the key to success in sex when you are stressed is to feel the need for intimacy. It is impossible to write a book on sexual intimacy without experiencing some along the path. If all couples sensed the urgent need for sexual intimacy and kept the goal and payoff in mind (a strong marriage that can weather any storm), then more couples would enjoy passion more often. Sometimes to get the spark a flyin' again, you need to remember back to why you first got married and how things were when you first fell in love.

THE NEWLYWED GAME

The first task of this eight-week project to fan the flame of your love is to remember back to when you were newlyweds. The day probably went like this:

Wake up (often by initiating sex).

Shower together (so if you didn't wake with sex, you made time for a quickie here).

Breakfast (if you had any time left; otherwise, grab a granola bar). Then you both run out the door, kissing. While you are kissing you are making plans for the next romantic rendezvous.

"Can you get home for 'lunch'?"

You worked frantically all morning because nothing, not rain, nor snow, nor sleet, nor anything else was going to keep you from your midday "snack."

You both zoom into the driveway and the minute you get inside the door (or maybe before on the sidewalk), you begin to shed clothes, and once the door is closed you tear at each other's zippers and buttons in a frenzy of passion.

You enjoy a quick romp and grab a peanut-butter-and-jelly sandwich to take with you in the car on the way back to work. Midway throughout the day you call each other with messages full of innuendo and remembrances of your magical times together while you make plans for the evening.

"Want to go to the gym and work out together or to the pool and swim and sit in the Jacuzzi?"

"Want me to make your favorite dish?"

"You are my favorite dish!" and you flirt back and forth enough to make everyone within earshot jealous by your obvious and open lovesickness.

The evening then may consist of a walk, a talk, a swim, or time in the Jacuzzi, or a romantic movie. You might cook together and feed each other because that's what lovers do. As newlyweds, you make time for foreplay and romantic and interesting conversation. Sex is relaxed and sleep comes easy because you both feel so terrific. Finally, you fall asleep content in each other's arms and wake up to begin the same wonderful routine all over the next day.

Who Stole Maui?

Why does this routine change? In a word, responsibility. The average couple doubles their level of responsibility every ten years, so by the time you are a midlife couple you are running everything:

- Running the kids to their numerous outside activities.
- Running the PTA, the church board, or the city council.
- Running your own corporation or someone else's.
- Running to meet friends, to the mall, to get the dog or yourself groomed.

- Running to care for your aging parents, the neighbor, or your best friend.

Life seems to catch couples running to everything except into each other's arms. While these are all good, worthwhile, and important activities, couples need to make each other something you run to regularly too.

Couples need T.I.M.E. together. Here is what we see as the minimum time commitment you should have to maintain (not to deepen or grow a relationship, but just *maintain the minimum* connectedness needed for a healthy strong marriage with little red-hot monogamy):

Ten to twenty minutes to talk together *alone* every day. (Time in the car with the kids listening doesn't count.)

Invest in a weekly date night (or date breakfast or lunch) together for at least four hours. (It takes a couple hours to emotionally connect, and then you want to leave at least a few minutes for sex.)

Make a monthly "day away" policy. At least once a month spend eight to twelve uninterrupted hours together to reconnect. You can spend the time doing things you *both* enjoy: errands, shopping, exercising, or a relaxing activity or hobby. Be sure you have the house alone (or at least your bedroom) for a few moments of red-hot monogamy sometime during this special day together.

Escape quarterly (or at least biannually) for a 48-hour weekend.

We'll give you some ideas and reasons why we think this is a nice formula for sexual success in this chapter and in the following chapters, but first we want a commitment from you two.

Will you give eight weeks of red-hot monogamy a shot? If so, both sign the commitment section below:

> I _____ (husband) do passionately commit to _____ (wife), and I _____ (wife) do passionately commit to _____ (husband) to make you the priority for the next several weeks, and I anxiously look forward to investing in our love life together and producing some red-hot monogamy.
>
> Signed:
>
> _____ (Husband)
>
> _____ (Wife)
>
> Date: _____
>
> Start of eight weeks of red-hot monogamy _____
>
> to end of eight weeks _____ .

STEPS TO BRINGING THE HONEYMOON HOME

If you are going to be successful at fanning the flame of love and romance, then there are a few simple steps you will want to take. First, let's look at our sample couple, Sol and Sunny. The first words of any book or movie often give a glimpse of the mood being established. How does Song of Songs begin? "Let him kiss me with the kisses of his mouth—for your love is more delightful than wine" (Song of Songs 1:1). This short sentence displays the longing, desire, and wishful hope of a wife wanting to be with her husband in an intimate way.

We will go more in-depth on how to handle it when you don't feel a desire for your mate or for sex in general, but for most people, it is common to go through phases of disinterest due to stress, business concerns, or emotional disconnection. Cathy was one woman who experienced this common issue. We so admired her solution that we offer it up to you as a great example of what to do when you sense the embers of your love growing cold:

> My husband and I were about to celebrate our ten-year wedding anniversary. I was holding down the fort while he worked full-time during the day, attended law school at night, and studied on the weekends. Halfway through this four-year commitment and weary from single-handedly parenting our four small children, something broke inside of me. Suddenly, my heart was empty. I no longer felt any love for my husband—a precious, godly man.
>
> I was honest with my husband about my dead emotions, and we seriously considered him quitting law school. However, after much prayer we decided to finish the course we believed God had called us to. We trusted that He would supply what we needed for our marriage and other responsibilities. We truly felt it was better to stay in the center of God's will, even though life was painfully difficult, than to face the consequences of stepping outside His will for our lives.
>
> By faith, day by day, I clung to my commitment to our marriage. But I was very vulnerable. In desperation I reached out for help from godly friends. These women were my mentors. They prayed with me and offered me wise counsel and supportive friendship. After several months I woke one morning with a glimmer of hope. I told my husband, "I feel a tiny sprout of love in my heart." Each day over the next several weeks my love grew little by little, until one day it was full grown in the garden of my heart.
>
> God was so faithful to answer our prayers and to fan the flame of love and desire for my husband again. I am blessed to say that I have been married to this wonderful man for more than 20 years now, and today

I am able to share with other young mothers how they too can fan and keep the flame of love in their own marriages.[4]

If you are not feeling very amorous, begin to pray that God would give you a renewed desire for your mate. I gave this counsel to pray for a renewed sex drive to one brave woman who was pretty disinterested in sex altogether, and she prayed, "God, give me the want to, to want to have the want to."

SETTING THE SCENE

Think back to your honeymoon. What was special about your surroundings that made it easy to be in love? It can be as easy as A, B, C.

A Is for Atmosphere

Have you been to a luxury hotel or spa lately? Have you ever been to a cozy cabin? A quick walk through any one of these places will give you a few pointers to help you set the stage for red-hot monogamy in your own home or apartment.

Privacy Provides Opportunity

You will feel freer to release, let go, and let your hair down if you have some privacy. Somehow create an oasis of your own. Unless you are nursing a brand-new baby, children should be in their own room. There is much controversy over "the family bed" theory in psychology, but if you want a marriage with red-hot monogamy, children should definitely not be present.

An inexpensive way to create privacy is to put in a stereo system that can play your favorite tunes. (Recently, while listening to the radio, we heard the DJ explain that people who listen to jazz have sex more often than the average couple. Of course, we were listening to a jazz station at the time!) However, know that as your children age, they may figure out the music camouflage. While driving with a friend and our teen children the title of this book came up. The daughter said, "Oh, I know when my parents have red-hot monogamy—the radio goes on!" (At least she has the benefit of two parents who are madly in love with each other.) Mom blushed a bit and said, "We've been thinking we should get a bigger house."

"Or a louder stereo!" piped in her daughter.

If you do have the opportunity to buy or rent a new home, be sure and check out the layout with red-hot monogamy in mind. Having your bedroom as a master suite is nice because a private bathroom adds much to intimacy possibilities. Next, see if you can create a little distance between your room and other bedrooms. A master suite wing is spectacular; however, one clever couple that couldn't change the floor plan decided to "decorate" their teen's room with soundproof panels because one of his walls butted up against the wall that held their bed.

Be sure to check the ventilation and heating systems. One couple thought they had planned their custom-built home well by placing their suite on the first floor of the home and all the kids' rooms upstairs. Years later at a family Christmas party after all the children were married, the now-grown teens revealed they chose to put on headphones at night because the air vents piped the sounds into their rooms from their parents' room. (So when purchasing a home, be sure to do the "shout test." Stand in your room and shout into the heating vents and see how far sound travels.)

Another way to enhance privacy is to see your bedroom as a love nest. Remove the desk, the laundry, the pile of books. (Okay, the book of *101 Greatest Romantic Poems* can stay.) It's hard to be romantic with your family finances basket staring you down from the corner or that undone term paper or business report sitting on a nightstand. Choose a closet or a screened-off area to create a mini office or a space for laundry or storage that is *not* in your bedroom. Make the bed so it is ready for intimacy. (But don't overmake your room. One wife had an all-white bedspread that her husband was not even allowed to sit on—that is a sure mood killer.)

The One-Eyed Monster

Should there be a TV in the bedroom? You might be surprised how often we are asked this question. Instead of an answer, let us ask you another question: Why do you want it there? If it is to avoid intimacy, to fill up the empty space where conversation should be, then we'd recommend you leave it in the living room. We didn't even own a television for our first year of marriage—on purpose, not just because we were poor college students. We even turned down offers for free TVs. The reason why is that we really wanted to set the foundation of being able to talk over all kinds of issues, so we wanted to make sure we had the time to talk.

One of the reasons we are so supportive of United Marriage Encounter is because they teach couples how to "dialogue." Couples take a simple question, write out their feelings, and then share them—and they do this every night. When we keynoted for the international celebration for Marriage Encounter, we were not at all surprised at the obvious affection expressed among the couples in the room. These couples had survived and even thrived amid life's storms to have marriages filled with red-hot monogamy because they have learned to communicate on a deeper level that richly enhances their love lives. So if you do decide to bring the TV into your room, dialogue on why it's there and what boundaries you want to set as a couple on what to watch and when to watch it. A romantic music concert might be a nice mood setter, but it's my guess that most women won't find their husbands playing the newest "Halo" video game as much of a turn on.

If you are going to have time for some red-hot monogamy, then you will need to turn off the TV. Dr. Paul Pearshall, author of *Super Marital Sex,* says, "TV addiction is one of the most detrimental influences on American marriages. It is a shared addiction, which is the worst type, because it sometimes covertly robs the relationship of available time for intimacy, while both partners take unknowing part in the theft."[5] Just for the next eight weeks, try turning off the tube.

B Is for Beauty

How can you bring some beauty in to set the ambiance for love? To set the right mood, you have to know what each of you thinks is beautiful, what is pleasing to your eyes. So here are a few questions to ask each other:

- What is your favorite color?
- What lighting sets the mood for you? (Bright and sunny? Candles? Colored lights? Small Christmas lights? Firelight?)
- What sounds arouse you?
- What aromas set your heart ablaze?
- What sights make your heart dance? A view? A sunset? The majestic? Quaint and cozy? Great art? Unique and eclectic?
- What styles do you prefer? Read a few of the many descriptions of a romantic getaway (your bedroom) listed below and see which kind of setting puts you in the mood.

Exotic Encounter

Have you ever wondered what any of these experiences would be like (or maybe you've had a few)?

- Sex under a natural waterfall

- Sex in the wilds of a jungle
- Sex on a beach
- Sex on a mountaintop
- Sex in a tree house ("You Jane. Me Tarzan.")
- Sex on the African plain
- Sex in a hut (perhaps in Thailand or one of the islands in the Pacific)

If any of these ideas spark more ideas in your brain, then you might be one who would enjoy a bedroom a little on the exotic side. You can create the right atmosphere in a variety of ways. Go for the Mosquito Coast look with a bed made out of bamboo. Hang a mosquito net over the bedposts or just as a canopy over the pillow area. Or go for the African safari look and use all kinds of animal prints and authentic (or authentic-looking) artifacts from the African continent. Or perhaps go for the island charm of Hawaiian prints, puka shells, and fresh plumeria. Create an outdoor shower open to the sky and place lush greenery inside the bed and bath area. Hang a hammock for two or get some wicker chairs to create a cozy setting for drinking Kona coffee while you relax with your feet in his lap.

Cozy and Quaint

If what turns you on is the thought of making love in a beach retreat on Cape Cod or along the sunny California coastline, then you are more amorous when the setting feels cozy or charmingly quaint. You might drift toward themes in decor with a home that is decorated in a beach or sailing theme, or perhaps a country French or shabby chic cottage appeal. If your dreams of romance include running in a field of daisies or making love in a country meadow, then you will feel more comfortable in a setting that makes you feel as though you are relaxing in Martha's Vineyard or in some quaint bed-and-breakfast (one that has good soundproof walls!). If you daydream of yachting, sailing, or flying in a two-seater, then your tastes in lovemaking will reflect a need for an atmosphere of a cottage at the beach.

Eden Experience

Some like sex in a more earthy way. If hot summer nights to you include a hike in the woods and stopping to make love on a rocky pinnacle or in some evergreen forest, then you long for a more Edenlike experience. Sex to you is more like it might have been when Adam and Eve roamed the earth. You prefer the fig leaf look in lingerie. Lovemaking daydreams might include a day relaxing in a canoe on a lake or canoeing to some secluded place to have sex. Sex and nature go hand in hand to you. Instead of strawberries and whipping cream as an appetizer, your form of food for lovemaking might include granola! You might even feel like a closet counterculturalist who is readier for sex when there are love beads hanging in the doorways and lava lamps and some tie-dye around to make your inner flowerchild awaken. You might long for the days of sex on a free-flow waterbed. Your blood may run hotter when you can capture the beauty of nature at home: a koi fishpond, a babbling brook, and plenty of plants and flowers complete with a serene green setting.

Simply Sexy

To some it is purely tacky, to others it is a total turn-on—the traditional trappings of Hollywood sexual settings. You know, a red velvet bedspread on a heart-shaped bed with a mirrored headboard (or mirrors overhead). Maybe a set of black leather sofas with mood lighting that can be dimmed with some sly snap of the finger or a simple "reach around the girl while shutting off the light" move. Red-hot monogamy might mean a wet bar with refreshments, an in-room hot tub, or a bearskin rug in front of the fireplace. Feeling in the mood might include the excitement of a setting like a weekend in a four- or five-star hotel: room service, a refreshing beverage bedside with two crystal glasses, and a view of city lights while you are 30 stories up. Sexy to you is framed in what might be seen on some Hollywood movie set—it has to have a bit of edge or glitz or you are just not in the mood.

Historic Hottie

To some, romance goes all the way back to the creation of what is now termed the Romantics. In literature, this term began during the days of King Arthur, Guinevere, Lancelot, and the rest of the Knights of the Round Table. To you, a perfect lovemaking getaway would be in a castle or an English country estate. Or move it forward a few centuries. Lovemaking to you might be capturing the romance of *Gone with the Wind* in its antebellum Southern setting, or at the very least, relaxing in some historic bed-and-breakfast known for its mark on history. You might feel more in the mood in some romantic European setting, in a gondola in Venice, dining at a sidewalk café and walking the art galleries of Paris, or taking in the sights of ancient Greece, or making love (or making pasta) in sunny Tuscany. You might visit Spain and consider the death-defying thrill of running with the bulls in Pamplona—that might be what makes you steam up inside. So add in some bold rustic red or hang some deep rich tapestry to add to the bedroom atmosphere.

Little Bit of Heaven

Perhaps sexual satisfaction is found easiest for you when everything is clean, pristine, pure, and well scrubbed. Romance to you is a spalike setting. You long for plush white robes, water with a twist of lemon, a good massage, and soaking in a milk bath with cucumber slices on your eyelids. For a lovemaking session, you'd want to shower together, have plenty of clean fresh towels to wrap up each other in, and fresh sheets, fresh flowers, and

soft instrumental music. To you, a padded lounge chair in the
sun is also a nice place to make love, provided there is a Jacuzzi
nearby and plenty of plush white towels! Your mind wants to be
completely relaxed in order to gear down from the cares and responsibilities of life and then be in the right frame of mind for
sex. If you are going for the floating on a cloud, slice-of-heaven
feel, then you're ready for a "relax all day, lounge around, and
spend the day in bed" kind of sex. No rush, no worries, just sex
and plenty of water and soft, clean towels!

Down to Earth

Some lovers are a bit more down to earth. Those with a bent
toward an affection for country music might also enjoy the look
of a cowgirl or a cowboy in tight jeans, the excitement of driving
in a full-sized pickup truck (and making love in it—or in the bed
in back). You might even be up for a roll in the hay or making
love after you have walked to the back 40. (If you don't know
what the back 40 is, you aren't this type of lover.) You prefer Willy
or Waylon or Hank playing on the radio for your lovemaking
sessions. A fantasy experience to you might include a horseback
ride to some secluded spot under an old oak tree or weeping
willow—or even a scrub cedar and then a quick lovemaking session under the open sky. You also might enjoy the picturesque
setting of a blanket for two down by the lake, with a picnic basket
you never quite get to.

Little Cabin in the Woods

For others, the smell of mountain air and a scenic valley view
from a mountaintop is a sure aphrodisiac. The smell of pine turns
you on. Lovemaking in a cabin tucked away down a dirt road
suits you just fine. You'd love to be snowed in for the winter with
the one you love. You get your lovemaking battery recharged by
building a redwood deck. A log cabin is your dream home. You

prefer your seating to be wooden rockers for two, an Adirondack chair, or a front porch swing. Handmade quilts spark romance. A ski chalet, a horse-drawn sleigh ride under a frosty moon, or even spending the day antiquing will prepare your heart for a night of lovemaking under a pile of covers. You probably own more wicker baskets than any one person should. Antlers, pine needles, and wood for the fireplace are tools that will create a romantic setting for you.

Walk on the Wild Side

Sturgis, South Dakota, a place on your road map for sex. You probably have a Harley or two parked in your garage. You might even have a black leather jacket hanging in your closet, if it hangs up at all. You live on the edge. You are, or want to be, part of the "mile-high club." (We fly all the time, and we have a hard time picturing how sex in one of those microscopic airplane bathrooms would be exciting—but to each their own...) You have probably enjoyed sex in the backseat of a car or sex in an elevator, or maybe even in a stairwell, hallway, or alley. You run the risk of public exposure and you like sex that way! The basic point here is that you like your sex a little on the edgy side. Bill and I are all for adventure in romance, and even a little risk; however, the payoff for hot sex should be marital intimacy, not dates with a parole officer. To keep yourself (or your spouse) out of the court system, bring your radical ways home. Decorate your love chamber with a black light or use vibrant colors, such as red. Talk through how to add the spark and sizzle in your decor in your bedroom so you aren't risking sex in places that could land you in jail.

Lover of the World

You are a world traveler. Maybe missions or maybe the military or maybe just for fun. Collect treasures from around the globe and use them to decorate your bedroom: Hang a kimono on a wall, light the room with Japanese lanterns, have a serving set from the Far East, and use furnishings from both Europe and Thailand in the same room. Hang a piñata or sombrero, place an ancient Inca figurine, and serve from teak bowls from Korea. Add in pictures you took while traipsing around the world on terrific tours and relive the memories of red-hot monogamy in different time zones. All those priceless treasures will remind you to make your love life a priceless treasure too.

If Unique Is What You Seek

If you don't fall into any of the above decor styles, then perhaps you march to the beat of a different accordion. One woman we know surprised her husband by renting a guard tower overlooking oilfields. She said the lights on the derricks going up and down were pretty. They spent the night camping about two stories off the ground in a round, open-air tower. It is also possible to rent a real lighthouse—but maybe your taste runs more to the ship at sea instead. If there is some unique place that is special to you, feel free to bring the joy home. One man we saw interviewed on late night TV made his bedroom look like a cabin of a sailing ship. (He made the bunks wide enough for two. We are sure his wife thought a double bed was a better idea than a traditional twin.) A NASCAR fan turned his bedroom into a shrine for a well-known driver. I am not sure how romantic his wife thought that was, but she was smiling on TV.

C Is for Communication

The point isn't so much what particular style you enjoy, but rather that you talk about what sets a romantic atmosphere for you. Every bedroom doesn't have to look as though Martha Stewart decorated it. Find your own style as a couple. Think through changes, major or simple, you might want to make your lover's abode more romantic. On our ten-year anniversary, we took an honest look at our bedroom and decided it was about time to actually invest in a bed with a headboard and footboard that expressed our style of love. One simple change we made recently was to add a sitting area with two comfy chairs and a coffee table so we can have a place to privately chat away from the listening teen ears that reside in our home.

Walk through your bedroom with the eyes of a real estate agent ready to list a home (or have a friend who is an agent do that and give you hints of things you might consider). How old is that bedspread, anyway? Want to clear the wrappers, cough medicine, and mail off the nightstand and place a picture of your spouse there instead? Do you really need three boxes of things to be filed in the corner? Don't they remind you of work instead of romance? Make preparations for sex, and you might find you are having a little bit more of it.

PREPARE A PLAN FOR PASSION

Every lofty goal, every great accomplishment in human history, every moment marked to remember began with a great plan. Those Apollo astronauts didn't walk on the moon by chance. If you want to make your love life soar, if you want to fly your spouse to the moon, then you too will want to have a plan.

There are a few tools of the trade you might want on your nightstand, or at least someplace in your bedroom.

Plenty of fresh towels. You can keep these tucked in a dresser drawer near the bed or in the nightstand. Where there is passion, there are fluids.

Mood lighting. Candles, a lighter dimmer, a pretty scarf to drape over the lamp, or even Christmas lights go a long way to set a nice hue for romance. (Here's a tip: Mood lighting does a lot to hide a messy room. It's hard to see the laundry basket in the corner with only a few candles glowing. It also makes you look thinner.

Oils, lotions, and potions. Have on hand massage oil, cocoa butter, and lotions. Experiment with what you like. If you are a newlywed or more than 50, you also might want some K-Y Jelly nearby to provide extra lubrication for her vagina in case of discomfort.

Sensational sounds. This can be your favorite artist playing on the stereo, or an instrumental CD, or even a sound maker that plays the sounds of a waterfall, rain, or the waves at the seashore. (We do not recommend leaving the news on; it's too depressing. *The Tonight Show* monologue is a maybe, but humor might be distracting. And please don't keep the movie on and watch over your mate's shoulder as he or she does the act...that is just plain rude. Give your spouse the present of your presence.)

Skin delights. You might want to invest in satin sheets, silk scarves, or even a feather boa. (Okay, we're getting close to the edge of the comfort zone for some of you.) However, the point is that some things just feel better on the skin, so talk about what you love touching you.

What about using other things, other ideas in bed...well, that's the next chapter. But before you go on, please take a moment to enjoy some red-hot monogamy.

Hands-on Homework

*L*ie on your bed together and take a look around your bedroom. Take a moment and explain to your mate which romantic decor style came closest to describing your preferences in a romantic setting. What ideas would you like to try to incorporate? Dream a little. You can get realistic and set a budget and list off the changes according to their priority later, but for now, wrap your arms around your spouse and talk about what atmosphere really turns you on. Then, set a goal this week for each of you to buy one item to be better prepared for red-hot monogamy.

Red-Hot ROMANCE IDEAS

26. Create a mailbox for love notes. Place it in your bathroom or on the kitchen table and exchange love mail. A traditional mailbox is nice because it has a red flag you can put up to signal "You've got mail!"

27. Burn a personalized CD of love songs that remind you of your love or the red-hot monogamy you have shared. Load some surprise songs onto his or her iPod.

28. Create a rhythm. Make love every full moon, take a walk every blue moon or harvest moon, try something new in sex the first day of every month. On the anniversary of your mate's birth date each month, make sex all about your mate. (For example, I [Pam] have a birth date of May 21, so that means on the twenty-first of every month, I get to choose what we do in the bedroom.)

29. Each of you take a blank set of Post-it Notes (each choose your own color) and write seductive, sensual things on each page, and then exchange the notes randomly. Place them on the mirror, the rearview mirror in the car, on his golf clubs, in her briefcase, inside his shoe, etc. Try to find the most outrageous spot to place the love note.

30. Each of you write out a list of ten free things that make you feel loved and exchange the list. Keep it handy in your organizer or Palm Pilot, and try to do one per day.

31. If you've never read romantic fairy tales, get a set of children's stories, such as *Snow White, Sleeping Beauty, Cinderella,* and *Rapunzel,* and read one each night for a

week. Then try to use lines from the stories in your daily life. For example, if you are in the mood for sex, you might say "(Your spouse's name), let down your hair!" Or each night before you go to sleep say to your spouse with a kiss, "And we lived happily ever after."

32. Play strip poker or strip Uno, checkers, or Yahtzee—any kid's game or card game will do.

33. Create a fashion show with your mate. Model some new sexy thing, complete with the runway walk and a commentary full of innuendo.

34. Do a slow seductive striptease with a sultry, sensual instrumental song in the background.

35. Personal delivery! Recruit friends or family or coworkers to deliver (1) a rose an hour from you. Have the first person bring a vase; (2) a series of handwritten love notes; (3) lines from love songs. For example, a coworker might walk up and say, "Bill just called to say 'I love you.'" "Bill says you are 'once, twice, three times a lady.'" "Bill said to tell you, 'Unforgettable, that's what you are.'"

36. Use everyday items to send a unique set of messages: The title of a candy bar with a note that says, "You are a Big Hunk of burning love" or "I am Red Hot for your love." See if you can work in all kinds of items: shaving cream, deodorant, perfume, cereal. (You are my "Life," etc.)

37. Place a picture of yourself in his or her briefcase, lunch box, on the seat of his or her car, or in an organizer.

38. Write a personal ad full of innuendo and place it in the local paper. (Don't put contact information in or you might get unwanted advances from others.) Circle it with a red pen and hand him or her the morning paper. Or

take out ad space and write a glowing ad full of praise for your mate.

39. Write your own "feature" article about your spouse, who was just named the "World's Greatest Lover." Include all their best traits as a lover, add in a picture of this famous lover, and frame it.

40. Use a magazine cover like *Time's* "Person of the Year" and scan in your spouse's picture. Or use *Glamour, GQ,* or another magazine with catchy headlines but replace the model with a picture of your mate.

41. Kidnap your spouse from work or some other responsibility—like in the middle of mowing the lawn—blindfold him or her, and then take him or her to a romantic rendezvous. (You might clear this with the boss or show up at the end of the workday. You don't want to get your spouse fired. That would definitely ruin the mood.)

42. Make a shadow box of memories: ticket stubs, seashells from your honeymoon, or postcards from vacation. Have a memory box or shadow box frame full of love.

43. For a month, make a file folder marked "Just for You" and tuck inside it articles, ads, game schedules, etc. you think your spouse might find interesting or helpful. After the month, hand your mate the file with these words written on the front: "I have been thinking of you every day. Here are a few things I came across that I think you might enjoy." (You can add in some tickets to their favorite sporting or theater event or a gift certificate to a spa or weekend away with you. It might take them a little while to find the surprise, so don't choose anything that is time sensitive.)

44. Buy a collector's copy of a favorite book, hunt down their favorite children's book from childhood, or send a copy of

a book by their favorite author to the author and ask the author to sign it.

45. Wrap a book or teaching video on romance, sex, or marriage in a provocative piece of lingerie. Add a note, "I want to keep the fire of our love red-hot."

46. Slide tickets to his or her favorite concert under his or her pillow.

47. Serve breakfast in bed with an invitation to spend the whole day there. Spend the day trying new things, napping in each other's arms, or playing a board game like An Enchanted Evening or Simply Romantic from Family Life Ministries.

48. Play Twister naked.

49. Send a care package to work. Toss in all your mate's favorite things: favorite foods and favorite comfort items (socks, hand cream, lip balm). You might add in a note, "Here are a few of your favorite things" and then add in a framed picture of yourself to the mix.

50. Meet some childhood dream. For example: Buy the horse he or she always wanted but couldn't afford. Get that collector doll or the whole set! Let him have the motorcycle his mom wouldn't allow. Find an unmet dream and meet it.

3

The Great Escape, Part 1

REST AND RELAXATION FOR ALL AREAS OF LIFE

Sometimes we long to escape for a little romance. Our friend Eva Marie shares this familiar feeling:

Remembering the hot steamy windows from making out in the backseat at the drive-in, one night my husband and I went parking to spruce up our sex life. Only we couldn't find anyplace to park. So we finally drove our car into the backyard behind our house. We climbed into the backseat and began to "neck," allowing one thing to lead to another...when all of a sudden a light shot through the darkness. We sat up and looked around. (It was like being caught by the

cops on Blueberry Hill!) There stood our 77-year-old
neighbor, Mr. C, spotting us with his flashlight from
just over the fence dividing our properties. We burst
out laughing and hit the floorboards as quickly as we
could. After a while, Mr. C went back inside—probably pretty perplexed. We did what married people
do, but we never really could look Mr. C in the eye
again.

It is healthy for couples to create a getaway tradition. We plan
a romantic getaway for our anniversary each year in December.
Then, because Bill's birthday is in March and mine is in May,
we select a date in April and go away to privately celebrate them
both. You can create a getaway to celebrate any date or event:
Groundhog Day, Valentine's Day, or any of the presidents' holi-
days. Perhaps more romantic for you are celebrations of the date
you met, your first kiss, or like our friends Brian and Marion, the
anniversary of your first date:

> The one thing my husband, Brian, and I have al-
> ways done is celebrate the anniversary of our first
> date, which is May 11. Sometimes we switch off who
> is going to do the planning, but generally Brian has
> made the plans. Early on we'd go to dinner, but as our
> youngest child grew older, Brian would surprise me
> with a weekend getaway, with all the plans made for
> our daughter's care included. However, a few years ago
> he really surprised me! I was checking my e-mail and
> there was one from Brian. He acted as he though he
> were a travel agent and was sending me my itinerary.
> He'd planned a wonderful trip for us to spend five days
> in Sedona, Arizona. This year, we just celebrated our
> twentieth first-date anniversary with a trip to the Big
> Island of Hawaii. Little did I know that for five months
> he was working with a jeweler, picking out diamonds
> and having a beautiful ring made. He surprised me the

first night we were there while sitting on the lava rocks
at our resort overlooking the Pacific. How blessed I
am to have such a romantic husband!

Yes, she is blessed. But, not to be outdone in romance by the
male gender, our friend Debbie, who is married to an officer in
the military, planned a grand surprise. Kevin is one of those guys
who would give you the shirt off his back and his last dime. He is
definitely one of the good guys. Since he is always such a blessing
to others, Debbie wanted to surprise him with the blessing of a
ten-day cruise for their anniversary. She arranged a cover story
with her mom about having to go to northern California to help
her parents plant trees. Then Debbie acted kind of disappointed.
"Oh, Kevin, it looks like we'll just have to put off any anniversary
celebration. My folks really need us to plant these trees. They are
getting older...they have done so much for us..." Debbie laid it
on thick, so Kevin, being the good son-in-law that he is, agreed to
go plant rows of trees. This took care of the need for luggage, and
it motivated Kevin to arrange the days off with his commander.

Debbie arranged with the cruise planners to have all corre-
spondence sent to her office address rather than to her home.
Debbie is the executive director of You Can! Ministries, so as the
cruise grew nearer, she drafted a letter on letterhead that said
the whole team and their spouses were to come to the docks at a
certain time, because the You Can! mentors (us), were going to
leave on their twenty-fifth anniversary cruise and the You Can!
team was going to all be there to send off the Farrels. This created
the reason to go to the cruise dock. Being the nice guy that he is,
Kevin was willing to stop en route to the tree planting to wave
good-bye. Finally, after they arrived at the docks and settled in
for breakfast, Debbie pulled out two tickets and their passports,
and told Kevin, "Happy Anniversary. We're going on a cruise!
Now!" Kevin's head was reeling when we saw him on board.

Those ten days were magical, especially considering he thought he was going to spend them planting trees.

Right Time, Right Place, Right Plan

We often think of a romantic getaway as a vacation to escape the responsibilities of life and get some rest. In reality, however, couples are wise if they look at all areas of their lives and set aside time to meet the key strategic need of that season. We are multifaceted human beings, and life occasionally throws in curves of change and roller coasters of rough circumstances. As a result, the kind of getaway you need this year may not be what you'll need next year. In addition, the couple who establishes a certain type of traditional getaway every year or two will experience more passion than those who wait for their interest to grow spontaneously. For example, we always try to get away for 24 hours to just recover physically after a book deadline. We always push ourselves and are sleep and fun deprived, so we head to a hotel with room service and nice workout facilities. We take off our watches (and our clothes) and sleep until our bodies wake us. We set no alarms. We eat when we are hungry. We enjoy one another sexually when we want to. The goal is to have absolutely no agenda.

Another consistent getaway we have included is part of our summer vacation. Sometime during our family vacation, most often the second day out because day one is sleeping and resting, I interview Bill about our life. We touch base on our ministry, family, and home goals. Once the year's plan is in place, I can relax, and that means Bill can relax.

There are many levels upon which a couple needs to build unity and intimacy. It is like looking at a diamond with its many facets. We are more than one dimensional in the way we, as couples in love, relate to one another. We suggest you develop intimacy in these areas:

- Social
- Financial
- Recreational
- Vocational
- Parental
- Emotional
- Spiritual
- Sexual

Social Intimacy

Have you ever experienced the magic of being alone together in a crowded place? Couples do it all the time: going out to dinner; having a cup of cappuccino at a sidewalk café; attending a movie, sporting event, or play; hitting the mall for some bargain hunting; dancing the night away on a cruise ship or at a wedding; or walking in the park on a Sunday afternoon. The world is filled with people in love!

There are benefits to going to a getaway spot that has a few other folks there than yourselves. The most obvious one is that it allows for choices. When getting away to a city or resort or cruise ship you can, at a moment's notice, decide between dancing, bowling, windsurfing, shopping, sightseeing, eating, eating, and eating.

This kind of getaway will serve you best when you, as a couple, just need a change of pace or a change of scenery. This isn't the kind of getaway you take to work out problems in your relationship (it might actually wake up or cause a few). And it isn't the getaway to do some serious work on your sex life, unless you plan on room service all weekend (so that's why you are headed to the five-star hotel).

A social getaway might be just the ticket if you are looking for a renewed sense of adventure or a way to expand your horizons or increase the level of interesting things to talk about. For example, for years Bill took missions groups to Mexico and later took our sons on a yearly fishing trip there. Meanwhile, I stayed home and nursed babies or held down the home front for the toddlers. Later, when the boys were older, we journeyed together to Mexico, and I, too, experienced the different culture, food, and ambiance south of the border. This connected Bill and me in a new way. We expanded our borders, and that made for some interesting conversations (and I picked up some pretty sexy sundresses along the way that my husband loves).

Take a moment and talk together about places you'd like to travel, things you'd like to see, and people you'd like to meet. Charlie "Tremendous" Jones once said, "What you are today is the result of the books you've read and the people you've met in the last five years." As a couple, discuss what kind of people you'd like to become and go do what those people do, see what they see, and read what they read. Go meet them!

Now that you have some idea of the trail ahead, add in the sexual dimension. Have you ever wanted to have sex in a hut, in a high-rise, or on a mountaintop? Each of you make a list of five places you'd like to have sex in or at. We still want to go to one of those secluded island paradises where the palapas have only wispy white curtains for walls and each little casa has its own private pool or spot on a secluded beach (oops…oh, yes, back to *your* sexual fantasy escapes…)

FINANCIAL INTIMACY

Do we have to talk about money? That's such a mood killer. We are aware of that. The number one topic married couples disagree over is money (or usually the lack of it). Money may not seem at all related to red-hot monogamy, but it is. You'll be glad you both set aside some time to really plan and prepare in the area of finances when you finally have saved up enough to head to Cancun, the Bahamas, Hawaii, Greece, Europe, or the Far East.

What could you do on a financial getaway that would lead to red-hot monogamy?

Crown Financial Ministries has some wonderful resources that can help you and your mate get on the same page financially. We bought *The Debt Diet* by Ellie Kay for all of our children. (We are saving a copy for our "still yet to go to college and face the real world" high school son.) In addition, if you are always under the gun every month, struggling to make ends meet or floundering under a mountain of debt, then a trip to a nonprofit agency that can help you negotiate a more effective and doable debt repayment plan will help you breathe again, and thus give you back a little life (as you trade worry for precious time together).

If you are struggling financially, now is not the time to splurge on some fancy getaway. Instead, see if some friends or relatives can take the kids for 24 hours. First, take time to pray together, and then take time to work through one of the financial resources listed above or head to the debt counselor. After that reward yourselves for creating a new budget or workable financial plan with a nice simple candlelit dinner at home. (Even mac and cheese or spaghetti looks more romantic under candlelight.) Draw up a bubble bath for two, maybe drink a little sparkling cider, turn on some romantic music, and dance your cares away. Sleep in late, have a simple breakfast in bed, and then make love all over again. We promise if you have sex twice in a 24-hour period, even the low checkbook balance won't suspend your smile. You don't have to be rich to have a sensational sex life. (If you look through the Red-Hot Romance Ideas throughout this book, you will notice that most of them cost nothing or very little.) Remember, we spent years pastoring a small church, and when we started writing books, it sure helped offset the cost of feeding three athletic sons. We have romance on a shoestring down to a science.

Here are just a few of our favorite ideas:

- Take a walk to a scenic view in your city.
- Bike to the park.
- Swing at the park and list off your mate's best traits A to Z.
- Check out a book from the library and read it together.
- Get a book of romantic poetry while at the library and read to each other.
- Have the dinner you were going to eat at the table on the rooftop instead.
- Go to the mall and try on free cologne and perfume.
- Play one of the kids' games (chess, checkers, backgammon, cards). The winner gets their choice of how to receive sex.
- Do free recreation: basketball or tennis at the park (or play badminton naked and use your bed as the net).
- Undress each other by candlelight to the tune of "your song."

Absolutely none of the above costs a dime (if you have the sports equipment for badminton sitting around, that is).

We have embraced these verses whenever we think about how to keep our sex life alive on a budget:

> Give me neither poverty nor riches, but give me only my daily bread. Otherwise, I may have too much and disown you and say, "Who is the LORD?" Or I may become poor and steal, and so dishonor the name of my God (Proverbs 30:8-9).

> Godliness with *contentment* is great gain (1 Timothy 6:6, emphasis added).

Just talking about how you can actually live within your means—or if you have plenty, setting a standard of living and then praying about how to invest, share, or give away the plenty—will help bring a sense of calmness to your relationship. If you are not always chasing the almighty dollar, or if you decide you don't want to keep up with the Joneses, this getaway will be well worth your time.

Kelly and Sam were one young couple that always seemed to be struggling. They were working two jobs each and never having time for one another while they did the tag team approach to parenting their toddlers. After a financial getaway, they decided enough was enough and they set in motion a plan to move from expensive Southern California to the Midwest, where housing prices were a fraction of what they were paying. In the heartland they found their pace and rediscovered the passion that produced their toddlers.

Bruce and Kate are a mature couple who are nearing retirement. After a weekend away, they decided to take the early retirement option at the company for which they both worked. They longed to spend retirement traveling and doing volunteer work while they were still young and healthy enough to enjoy it.

Just taking a hiatus and calling a time out will help you gain some perspective. In our own life, on a missions trip to Europe to minister to the military, we noticed that Europeans enjoy a much different pace than we are accustomed to. They take an average of 18 to 35 vacation days per year, compared to our 10 in the States.[1] Every Sunday in Germany, there are quiet laws with no mowing of lawns, cutting down trees, or the like. Instead, you will find people walking or bicycling through the beautiful woods or swimming in one of their expansive recreational swimming facilities with all kinds of pools and Jacuzzis. Although we agreed we would probably not want to slow down to the pace we saw in Germany, the trip did cause us to set a date for a getaway to talk through the second half of our lives.

In this conversation about sex and money, you have to hear some recent research out of Dartmouth College:

> Good news for folks whose bedrooms have more activity than their bank accounts: Research shows that sex is better for your happiness than money.
>
> That's not to say that being financially poor but sexually active is the secret to a happy life. But despite common theory, more money doesn't get you more sex, say "happiness economics" researchers.
>
> After analyzing data on the self-reported levels of sexual activity and happiness of 16,000 people, Dartmouth College economist David Blachflower and Andrew Oswald of the University of Warwick in England report that sex "enters so strongly (and) positively in happiness equations" that they estimate increasing intercourse from once a month to once a week is equivalent to the amount of happiness generated by getting an additional $50,000 in income for the average American.
>
> "The evidence we see is that money brings some amounts of happiness, but not as much as what economists might have thought," says Blanchflower. "We had to look to psychologists and realize that other things really matter."
>
> Their paper, "Money, Sex, and Happiness: An Empirical Study," recently published by the National Bureau of Economic Research, essentially puts an estimated dollar amount on the happiness level resulting from sex and its trappings.
>
> Despite popular opinion, they find that having more money doesn't mean you get more sex; there's no difference between the frequency of sex and income level. But they do find sex seems to have a greater effect on happiness levels in highly educated—and

presumably wealthier—people than on those with lower educational status.

Overall, the happiest folks are those getting the most sex—married people, who report 30% more between-the-sheets action than single folks. In fact, the economists calculate that a lasting marriage equates to happiness generated by getting an extra $100,000 each year. Divorce, meanwhile, translates to a happiness depletion of $66,000 annually.[2]

We think whatever you paid for this book was money wisely invested.

Recreational Intimacy

Year after responsible year, couples can forget how to have fun together. Recently we were reminded of the term "recreational intimacy" on a double date with a pastor and his wife in which we went "tubin'" (inner tubing) down the Chattahoochee River. The day was spent floating (and sometimes hanging on for dear life in the rapids). It was flat-out fun. When was the last time you and your spouse:

- Square-danced
- Ballroom danced
- Danced under the stars
- Took a walk in your neighborhood
- Hiked a trail
- Canoed or kayaked
- Boated, water-skied, or sailed
- Bicycled
- Flew a kite
- Walked the beach
- Walked around a lake

- Skateboarded, snowboarded, or snow-skied
- Snowmobiled
- Motorcycled or off-roaded in a four-wheel-drive
- Rode a horse
- Rode in a carriage, sleigh, or on a hayride
- Snow-sledded or tobogganed
- Inner-tubed down a river or in the snow down a hill
- Ran or jogged
- Worked out at an athletic club (at the same time)
- Lifted weights while you spot each other
- Jumped on a trampoline
- Jumped out of an airplane
- Took an aerobics class
- Took a Pilates or stretch class
- Took a hula class
- Snorkeled or scuba dove
- Windsurfed (or surfed or boogie boarded)
- Cowboyed
- Rock climbed
- Jumped rope
- Played hopscotch
- Twirled a baton or spun a hula hoop around your hips
- Played basketball, touch football, soccer, or tennis
- Did a cartwheel or stood on your head

It is wise to work in a weekly *active* date into your life. To kick-start a more active love life, you might want to take a more active weekend getaway (or longer) vacation. Endorphins play a huge role in our emotional wellness and happiness. If you are physically active, your body produces more endorphins and, as a result, you will just feel happier and more interested in sex as an activity!

There is a positive correlation between sex and sports according to a BBC article. "[Sex] The night before has no effect on strength or endurance or any of the physical abilities of the athletes," says physiology expert Dr. Ian Shrirer, a former president of the Canadian Academy of Sport Medicine.[3] Israeli physician Alexander Olshanietzky notes, "We believe that a woman gets better results in sports competition after orgasm...Generally, it's true of high jumpers and runners. The more orgasms, the more chances of winning a medal."[4]

"Research suggests that people who get regular aerobic exercise have more sex, better orgasms...than nonaerobic exercisers," says James White, Ph.D...Possible reasons: Vigorous exercise may increase natural testosterone levels (which might fuel desire in women as well as men), and it helps pump blood down to erogenous zones, like the vagina, increasing sensation. Regular workouts also boost your energy (remember, good sex can be hard work!), improve your confidence in your appearance and confer a sense of general well-being, all of which can give your libido a lift."[5] Seventy-eight sedentary men were studied over nine months as they began to exercise sixty minutes a day, three times a week. Every single man noted increased frequency, performance, and a greater level of satisfaction in his sex life.[6]

Take out your Palm Pilots and organizers and schedule in a little fun activity this week. (It's a performance enhancer, after all.) You might also decide a recreational intimacy getaway is just what the doctor ordered. If so, mark off a little vacation time. Get out those travel brochures, and figure out where you want to go play again.

VOCATIONAL INTIMACY

If you thought the financial getaway was off the romance trail, what you're probably thinking right now is, "How can talking about work help our love life?" It can't—so just move on.

Just kidding! What happens to many couples is they work so much, they never talk about why they work so hard, what they are working for, or how they will use their little bit of free time when they do have it. Sometimes couples become overly focused on their careers because they have never gotten on the same goal plan sheet. Or maybe there are issues that need addressing in their relationship that feel too complicated, so more work seems easier than dealing with the problems.

Once a year (or at the very least once every 18 months), Bill and I go away to talk about the work/ministry side of our life and family. We have always been very proactive in the area of setting ten-year, seven-year, five-year, three-year, and one-year goals for our individual lives, for our careers, for the ministries we run, and for our family and home. However, it was on a date that we decided this deliberate approach was vital. In the midst of an amazing romantic environment, we watched a couple have an emotional meltdown before our very eyes. They began talking about money issues on this romantic interlude, which soon turned into a dramatic scene, complete with yelling and crying. We prayed for this couple and then looked at each other and said, "Let's make sure that is never the story of our life!" That night we became even more convinced of the necessity of being on the same page in the area of goal setting. The business of life had stolen this couple's red-hot monogamy, and we vowed to not let that happen to us.

On a goal-setting weekend, to really be clear minded, you will need to begin and end with five things:

1. *Prayer.* You need to hear God's voice leading you louder than anything else.

2. *Rest.* Take a nap before you dig in and discuss. Then take a nap as a reward before you go home and face real life again.

3. *Good food.* Cook together or eat at a favorite romantic spot when you begin and end this getaway. In our book *Why Men and Women Act the Way They Do,* we ran across research that said men are happier after they eat. At the same time, the place in a woman's brain that controls eyesight is stimulated. She becomes more aware of her life, and he is more willing to engage her. So folks, the way to a man's heart and the way to better interaction really is around the table. If you have a tough topic to discuss with your husband, feed him a great meal, give him super sex, and then share what's on your heart.

4. *A little activity.* Do something simple. A 20-minute walk or swim will clear your brain and replenish you.

5. *Great sex.* Set an amount of time for talking about, writing down, and processing your goals and work discussion. Reward yourself with sex by each selecting one of the Red-Hot Romance Ideas to do before you get in the car and head home. (Remember, we said do these things at the beginning and end. At the beginning, reward yourself with sex just for making the effort to go on this kind of goal-oriented getaway.)

PARENTAL INTIMACY

After money, the second-leading cause of arguments in marriage is decisions over the kids. This is especially true with the challenge of blended families. We often speak at family camps, where the topics in the adult sessions range from marital issues to how to discipline and motivate children and teens. There are a few vital times we suggest you get away to get on the same parenting page.

Before the birth of your first child. You will want to talk through how you were each raised. What things do you agree with and what things do you want to change? What is your parenting philosophy? Books such as *Growing Kids God's Way, Discipline Them, Love Them,* and much of the work of James Dobson, FamilyLife Today, and Kevin Leman can help you define your philosophy of parenting. Philosophy simply means the "how" of raising children. Our philosophy of parenting is found in *The 10 Best Decisions a Parent Can Make* and *Got Teens?* Because we took time early to get on the same page in our parenting philosophy, we rarely disagree in this area.

Before your first child enters school. Life is about ready to change. Children will pick up their own social life, activities, and schedules. Which one of you will manage science fair, math homework, or teaching them to do chores? At what level will you be involved in your church's children's ministry or as a volunteer in the community? Will you coach soccer, head up a parent-teacher organization (PTO) board, or help run the Fall Festival on October 31? Talk about how much time and energy you can each donate to your children's lives and activities. You have a responsibility to give to those groups that are giving to your children, so your biggest question should be, "How much do we do individually, and how much do we commit to together as a couple or as a family?" And how will you keep your romantic life alive? Will you have weekly date nights? Weekends away? Vacations? Who arranges child care for these things?

Before your first child enters their teen years. Now life is really going to change. Your schedule will move into warp speed, especially during the high school years. You *must* be on the same page in your answers to your teen on how you will deal with dating, discipline, drinking, drugs, dances, and all the other dilemmas that crop up during the teen years. If you took the time to lay a strong foundation, the teen years can be a delight as you see your teen blossom into an incredible and grounded young adult.

The biggest challenge to your red-hot monogamy at this stage of life is privacy. Your bedtime is probably before your kids'. How do you have sex if in the next room more than 15 teens are eating pizza? You will need to create some private space in your home and private time in your schedule. Take advantage of those Friday and Saturday nights when the kids are all out at a movie. (Just be sure you get the movie time accurately from your teens so they don't walk back in the house with their six friends and catch you with your pants down (literally). They are now old enough to arrange to stay with friends when you go out of town. Take advantage of this. Don't be afraid to tell your teens that you are going away for romance. They will probably be embarrassed, but inwardly they will be proud of you.

Before your first child leaves home for college or career. This is the launching pad. Your empty nest emotions may surprise you. There are many areas of potential disagreement too. In the teen years there were allowances, decisions about who pays for what when they start driving, etc., but now the stakes are upped There are college bills, rent, and weddings. Be sure to talk issues through privately before you meet with your adult child. As the last one flies from the nest, you might look at each other and ask, "Now what? We've been spending all our time with the kids. What do we do with this free time?" Or you might ask, "Who are you?" The responsibilities of life will change us, so you may need some extended time together to become reacquainted. Some helpful books at this stage of life are *The Second Half of Marriage, Fighting for Your Empty Nest Marriage, The Act of Marriage After Forty,* and *Why Men* and *Women Act the Way They Do.* Words like "Viagra," "K-Y Jelly," and "hot flashes" might become part of your vocabulary as the sex act changes with age. The upside is you can go on adventures because no on is waiting for you at home. Those trips to your kid's college weekends can also be mini second honeymoons.

Before your first grandchild. Along with the joys of being a grandparent are a few challenges. How will it impact you emotionally to be called "Grandma" and "Grandpa"? Short skirts are long gone, so what clothes are "sexy" now? How much time will you devote to your grandchildren? If they live away from you, how often will you visit and how often will they visit you? This is also when the reality of your mortality hits. Are your affairs in order for your mate should your health fail? Are you financially ready for retirement?

This is also a time when love is the sweetest and most poignant. In the movie *The Notebook*, we see a husband fighting to stay emotionally connected to his wife, who has Alzheimer's. He daily reads to her their love story out of a notebook. Sometimes her mind clicks back into reality and she responds. Those few brief moments make all the hours of reading worthwhile.

What's the next natural life transition on the road ahead? Is it time to plan a getaway to better prepare for this life stage?

Hands-on Homework

*O*ne of our favorite stories of a marriage ritual was one couple that decided that every time they made love, they would put a dollar in the bank and save toward their second honeymoon. Often he'd walk in from work and say, "I've got a dollar!" and she'd respond, "I know how to spend it!" Then off they'd go to the bedroom. This ritual happened week after week for years. If a business meeting would turn boring, all she had to do to end the meeting was to slide a dollar bill across the table—business meeting *over*. Year after year they traded dollar bills back and forth, enjoyed satisfying sexual intimacy, and watched their money add up in the bank. When their fiftieth wedding anniversary came around, they went to Hawaii for several weeks and stayed in the best places, ate at the nicest restaurants, and enjoyed the most exciting adventures and activities. On their return home their daughter picked them up at the airport. Later she said, "At baggage claim Daddy pulled out his wallet, took out a dollar, and said to Mama, 'Want to start saving for Cancun?'"

What do you want to save for? Having sex is like making a bank deposit that grows with interest. When times get tough in your relationship, you have a relational romance reserve to draw on.

Sex in itself is a reward for a solid intimate relationship, but staying "in the mood" requires an investment of time. Which kind of escape away do you need more of? Check the list below:

- A daily time to talk
- A daily have fun/be active time
- A daily spiritual moment together (prayer, Bible reading, reading a devotional)

- A weekly "business side" of life and family time
- A weekly date
- An extended weekend (or even 24 hours away together)
- A real vacation alone together

Now create an incentive plan or a tangible reminder (like a dollar taped to the mirror) so you can remember to work this new intimacy connection into your schedule.

Once you have decided, reward yourselves with a little red-hot monogamy.

Red-Hot ROMANCE IDEAS

51. Toss it. Is there a habit your spouse wants you to break? Maybe it is something more tangible, such as an old T-shirt she hates, some old gym shoes that reek, an ugly old chair from your college dorm. As a love gift to your mate, toss out something he or she hates.

52. Recycle something you hate but they love. Recover that old chair, frame and mount that high school jersey, make a display case for that collection of NASCAR programs. If something has been sitting around the house for a while, there might be a reason, so instead of fuming, turn what seems to be trash into a treasure.

53. Buy a mini frig or ice bucket for your bedroom and keep some chilled treats on hand. (Whipping cream, strawberries, marchino cherries, some favorite beverages, etc.)

54. Wash each other's hair (or each other's bodies).

55. Put in a two-headed shower stall.

56. Replace the tub with a Jacuzzi tub for two.

57. Take a whole day to do all the things that your sweetie never seems to get around to. (Take the dog to the groomer, wash the windows, change all the lightbulbs, head to the dry cleaners, water the plants.)

58. Have dinner someplace different in your home: in front of the fireplace, on the rooftop, on the patio or balcony out back, in the attic, under the tree in the backyard.

59. Create a luau in the living room. Borrow some plants, get some island music, throw down some beach towels, bring in luau food, and wear your sarong or skimpy bathing suit.

60. Share a banana split or milkshake, make one bowl of pasta but bring two forks, split some sensuous scrumptious chocolate dessert, share a stick of gum by placing one end in your mouth and daring your mate to bite off his or her half with a kiss.

61. Create a massage experience. (Get a book or attend a class to learn some techniques.) Then lower the lights, add in soothing music and massage oils, and let nature take its course.

62. Do a mini massage. Rub your mate's shoulders, feet, hands, hair, and head or neck. Give one another a foot rub at the same time by placing your feet in each other's laps.

63. Take a bubble bath together. Remember glasses of sparkling grape juice or other yummy treat, fresh fruit, candles. And definitely take the time to pat your mate dry as you exit the tub.

64. Meet me mystery. Leave a message on voice mail or e-mail inviting your spouse to "Meet me at _____ (time) at _____ (place), and don't forget your _____ (passport, tennis shoes, toothbrush, silky red dress)." Try to keep the actual date, location, and activity a secret.

65. Create a secret signal or verbal code for "I want some red-hot monogamy, pleeeeease." Use the code word or silent signal in public as often as possible!

66. Wear a dress and forget your panties. Wait till you are out on a date to whisper that vital info into your husband's ear.

67. Buy or create a relationship coupon book. Put in coupons for: one night of red-hot monogamy (your choice of positions), one free back rub, one dinner of your choice, one back scratch, one foot or neck rub.

68. Go through your spouse's purse, suitcase, or jacket pockets and leave love notes to be found throughout the year or throughout a trip.

69. Get one of those alarm clocks on which you can record a message. Record a wake-up call that will not only get him or her out of bed but may find you back in bed together!

70. Write something romantic on a roll of toilet paper or paper towels and reroll.

71. Leave love notes between the pages of a book or magazine your mate is reading.

72. Record a video message for your mate but then label it as a movie and put it in a movie box. Sit down with popcorn, a cozy blanket, and then play "the surprise feature" for your spouse. Don't watch the real movie until there has been an intermission for some red-hot monogamy.

73. Make a public statement of your love. Rent a billboard, hang a sheet over a freeway overpass, make a banner for the garage door, write in chalk on the driveway, paint on a wall that you are going to be repainting anyway. One year for Valentine's Day, I hung hot pink posters all around town in the places I knew Bill would go. They had messages like: "You are hot." "You are incredible." "You are amazing (spectacular, one in a million)." They went above the coffeepot, on his windshield, on the front door of the church where he worked, on his office door, on the basketball equipment he used for coaching, on the front door

of our home, on the garage door, on the shower door, on the foot of the bed, and on his pillow.

74. Buy a blank puzzle and write a message, or take poster board, write a message, and then cut it into puzzle-shaped pieces. This can also be done with a provocative photo of you or a romantic picture of the two of you with an invitation to a date on the back.

75. Use inexpensive dime-store Valentines to create a trail of clues that lead to a romantic destination. You can also make this into a car rally by taping the Valentines around town, around the mall, or leave taped to your friends' front doors. For a different spin on a surprise party, leave the clue with friends who first compliment your mate, give him their own gift, and then add in a verbal or written clue that leads them to the next friend.

4

The Great Escape, Part 2

REJUVENATING AND REENERGIZING LOVE

My friend Kristy wanted to wow her spouse one day:

One evening I decided to create a romantic atmosphere in the bedroom. It was very appropriate because I'd had a virus, and it'd been several days since…(you know!). While Milton was in the shower, I slipped on a slinky black ooh-la-la, folded the covers down to the foot of the bed, lit a candle, and sprayed perfume on the sheets. As a final touch, I clicked on the bedside radio for some soft background music and then lay down, posing pleasingly. Just as Milton walked into the bedroom, a deep bass voice belted out on Christian radio, "How long has it been?" Needless to say, the atmosphere changed from romantic to hilarious as we burst out in laughter. However, it quickly changed back.

As couples, we long to reconnect. One couple shared, "We know our kids know we have up close and personal time. They have nicknamed it 'The eleven o'clock click' because the lock on our door makes a distinctive sound that can be heard through most of the house."

If you long to get behind closed doors, here are a few more types of connections you will want to schedule in.

EMOTIONAL INTIMACY

The goal of this kind of time-out is to reconnect conversationally so it will become natural to reconnect sexually. Married couples can often become two ships that pass in the night. I once told Bill (who was a senior pastor at the time), "Enough is enough! The last three dates I have been on with you were to funerals. Something is wrong with this picture."

If you discover that your time together recently has been focused around Home Depot or the kids' soccer games, it might be time for a little change. Given the pace of life today, a wise couple should learn to use their time twice. Learn to make going to Home Depot, the kids' soccer games, or even a funeral a romantic journey. We made something as tragic as a funeral meaningful by asking each other questions such as, "What do you want to accomplish before you die?" "What do you want said about you at your funeral?" "What do you want the service to be like?" Those questions are on the serious side, but they connected our hearts at a deep level. Discussing dreams and hopes during trips to the home improvement store will lead to intimacy, as can a van ride with the kids in tow as you talk over your plans for their futures. The journey can be the part of the date that sets you up for red-hot monogamy later because now you are emotionally in tune and entwined.

Our dear friends Larry and Jo-Ann have one of the happiest and healthiest marriages we know of. Their fond affection, respect, and desire for each other emanates from them both. We asked Jo-Ann the secret, and she put it so well, we'll let her tell you:

> I have been getting up before five AM for 32 years to make Larry lunch and breakfast. Last year, when I went back to work full-time, Larry started making my lunch on Fridays. I really look forward to those days and feel that I am loved when I open up that lunch and look forward to seeing what he has put in it. It is such a simple thing, and yet it shows the love and appreciation he has for me. This example is not incredibly romantic or creative, but it speaks of love, commitment, and caring to me.
>
> Another example of how we keep connected is just being together. For example, several weeks ago we got up early and drove down to the Torrey Pines Preserve. We spent several hours hiking the trails, talking, and enjoying God's beautiful creation. Then we drove down the coast and had breakfast at an outdoor café in Encinitas. We talked about our plans, fears, children, hopes, disappointments, past joys and let downs, and dreams. It was a wonderful day of sharing our love and joy at being together. As we relived our accomplishments and failures, we marveled at how God's presence has guided us to this point in our lives. That day will always be one of my best memories of our lives together.
>
> The thing that makes me love Larry more than anything is his unfailing support, encouragement, and confidence in me. He truly believes that I am the most beautiful and sexy woman alive, even though I can never believe that for myself. He believes that I am smart and capable, even though I struggle with feeling

inferior. He is certain that I *am* a Proverbs 31 woman, even though I feel that I have and will always fall far short of that mark. Yet, through the eyes of his love, I believe more and more each day that I am all these things and more. What a miracle that someone on this earth loves me that much.

Whenever Bill and I are at their home, we never feel rushed or pressed. Their love reminds us of a key romance principle. Sometimes you just need to "be" together. You know, lie together in a hammock or next to each other on a beach towel. Curl up on the sofa and watch the fire or sit side by side on a front porch swing. Share a lounge or Adirondack chair and a soda or iced tea. Drift in a canoe as you lie across each other's legs. Sometimes you will want to just soak in the silence together.

Other times you will want a quiet afternoon, a long car ride, or stroll to include some conversation. Sometimes there is a need to just get away and talk so that reconnection happens emotionally. It is much easier and more natural to reconnect sexually when you are connected emotionally.

This is often a challenge for couples because the wife has access to a lot more words than her husband. When a disconnection is happening, it is usually the wife who says, "Honey, we need to talk." Her husband looks at her with a blank expression and says in sincere surprise, "About what?"

That's why in this book, and in all the books we write, we offer conversation starters that might prompt some discussions in new areas of interest, or deeper discussions on vital topics.

Here's a simple one related to this topic. "Of all the places on earth, where is your favorite place to 'be' with me?"

Spiritual Intimacy

Attending to your spiritual life can directly impact your sex life. Check out this underreported study. Religious women were most satisfied with the frequency of intercourse, felt free to discuss sex openly with their husbands, and were more orgasmic than the nonreligious women.[1] Why would a deep, rich, spiritual life bond two people in their intimate life?

Prayer is intimate. We travel a lot, and we really appreciate hotels that have the small peek holes so that when someone knocks you can see who's there. That is what prayer is like. People usually aren't phony when praying because it is a time of vulnerability before God. Couples that pray together get a window into each other's hearts. You might feel irritated at your spouse all day, you might not understand why she did or said something, but during prayer you get to see what was really going on in her life, her thoughts, and her heart. Prayer gives us a deeper understanding of our mate. Anything that gives a deeper understanding will deepen intimacy. Deeper intimacy creates the safety net for a nakedness of the soul, and if you are in a place where you both feel comfortable when your soul is naked before each other, then the physical nakedness of sex is an easy logical next step in the sharing of your lives.

Reading the Bible is intimate. The Bible is God's love letter to *each* of us. If you know your spouse is listening to God, your trust level will grow. If you notice that your spouse is seeking to follow the commands of God, you will feel more relaxed when you are together. God has a complete love for you, and when God has your mate's attention, God will steer your spouse into making more loving choices toward you. As a result, the nagging rate naturally diminishes. And less nagging and negative corrective language and more positive affirming language is the cultivated, fertile ground of a great sex life.

The influence does not stop with your spouse, however. If you are reading the Bible and praying, God will have *your* attention and make *you* a better lover. His love will flow through you to a grateful spouse.

The Holy Spirit is intimate. When we know Christ personally, the Holy Spirit resides in us and gives us supernatural power to love. It is a supernatural power so that we can love, not just with our power, but with God's ability. And since the Holy Spirit indwells anyone who asks Jesus into his or her life and He knows the way your spouse was designed to be loved, you have the ability to become a great lover for your mate. You will notice that the Holy Spirit gives very specific instructions. He makes it simple enough that your only choice is to obey or disobey. In our life, it may sound something like this:

> *"Pam, what you said just now to Bill was unkind. He really is a good man, and he deserves a gentle response."*
>
> *"Bill, go home. Pam needs you. Do not do that next task; leave right now."*

Intercourse is a spiritual act. In addition to the love lessons that God provides, the very act of intercourse is spiritual. Genesis 2 contains the story of the very first marriage. It is obvious from the very beginning that this is a relationship of spontaneous emotional energy and sexual passion. God put His endorsement on the sexual union of a man and his wife when He said, "For this reason a man will leave his father and mother and be united to his wife, and they will become one flesh. The man and his wife were both naked, and they felt no shame" (Genesis 2:24-25). The discussion is intensified in Ephesians 5. The apostle Paul compares the relationship between a man and wife with the love between Jesus and the church. He quotes from Genesis 2 when he writes, " 'The two will become one flesh.' This is a profound mystery—but I am talking about Christ and the church (Ephesians 5:31-32). A couple is never more "one flesh" than in the act of sexual intercourse, so, even though it seems incomprehensible when we say it, every time a married couple enjoys one another sexually, the gospel is proclaimed!

How can you create mini spiritual retreats?

Daily

Each have a daily quiet time. Read the Bible or a daily devotional and pray alone. Then come together to discuss what God taught each of you. (Our daily devotionals *Devotions for Women on the Go* and *Devotions for Men on the Go* help you grow with God in just five minutes a day.)

Have devotions together. There are couple's devotional Bibles and books. Our study guide for *Men Are Like Waffles—Women Are Like Spaghetti* is an example of a couple's Bible study.

Pray over each other. We pray together and then kiss after grace at each meal. We pray over each other quickly as we head out the door each morning. We call each other for prayer when we hit snags in our day. We pray over each other as we lie in bed before we nod off to slumber. (Here's a clue, you've prayed too long if you hear snoring.) Prayer is like the duct tape of great sex. It'll hold you two together through anything.

Prayer walk together. We have witnessed firsthand in our own life, and in the lives of other couples who practice this disciplined date, the joy and intense intimacy that happens when you daily walk and pray together.

My brother, Bret, and his wife, Erin, walk four miles each morning to welcome the dawn. Before they started prayer walking, three active kids, as well as community and church involvement, had them in "contestant mode." Rather than working together, they were competing with one another over whose agenda would win out. The prayer walk became their place of connection. That connection deepened. To be around them now, you would think they were newlyweds. They kiss all the time, hang on each other, and love to retire to bed early. I believe the result of all those early morning prayer walks created an incredible connection. Bret and I grew up in a very dysfunctional home because my father struggled intensely with alcoholism and rage. Bret has worked hard not to repeat any of the negative patterns we witnessed while growing up. We'll let Erin pick up the story from here:

As our twenty-first wedding anniversary approached, Bret and I had agreed to not give gifts this year. Our eldest daughter, Rebekah, was to graduate from high school in just a couple of days, and we had already gone on an expensive-but-fun cruise celebrating the joint-but-seperate anniversaries of our sister and brother-in-law (their twenty-fifth and our twentieth) in January. So with the money already spent, I was hoping for a quiet evening of just the two of us.

However, Bret surprised me. He had contacted a neighbor who is a silversmith, and arranged for her to make me a Western belt buckle. It was beautifully engraved and on it had our wedding date and our twenty-first anniversary date (6-2-84; 6-2-05). Bret came to pick me up from a school meeting, and when I climbed into the truck, there was the beautiful belt and custom-made buckle. I *cried!* Then I said, "Honey, I love it, but why? We agreed to not get presents for each other." Bret proceeded to tell me that this anniversary was very important to him. He remembers spending his parents' twenty-first anniversary with his mom at the local KFC—no dad present. That was his parents' last anniversary. They divorced before their twenty-second. It was a milestone in Bret's life that we not only reached our twenty-first but spent it together—loving each other even more on June 2, 2005, than we did on June 2, 1984. It's praise to the goodness and faithfulness of God and to the love of a wonderful man who determined and desired to make his marriage a success. Bret successfully made the junk of his childhood stop with him.

Weekly

Attend a small group Bible study for couples. Create an evening out that includes dinner, Bible study, and coffee or dessert afterward. Or work out together and then head to Bible study. Couples that are part of friendship circles that believe in long-term, red-hot monogamy tend to have red-hot monogamy for the long term. (We are what we believe.) And when couples hit a crisis, friends are around who can say, "Hang in there. You two will make it." Too often, when a marriage hits rough waters, the guy starts hanging out with his single buddies and the woman with her single friends. Some of those singles might have just experienced divorce, so it is easy for the "Men are scum" and "All women are witches" attitudes to rub off. Now what was a temporary issue can become a permanent problem. So if your red-hot monogamy has cooled to freezer level, both of you need to run to couples who have hung in there.

Attend church. Consider going out to breakfast before or lunch after the service to extend the date time. You can deepen the experience by volunteering to serve God while at church. Your pastor will have numerous options available that line up with your gifts, talents, and available time. Serving God together adds a deeper dimension to your sex life. As your hearts connect to ministry together, that is one more bond that ties them together. Then every ministry experience you have, every life you impact, every answer to prayer you see is another connection. Person after impacted person, experience after spiritual experience creates a wonderful web of unity at the deepest level. A couple whose hearts are tied that closely together will experience more red-hot monogamy.

Yearly

Conferences. We take our cars in for regular tune-ups, seed our lawns, and paint our houses because important things in life need a little TLC. Surely our relationships are of greater value than a car. There are several places to learn about good Christian marriage conferences: FamilyLife Today, Marriage Alive, Masterful Living, United Marriage Encounter, and Marriage Savers. Smart Marriages, www.smartmarriages.com, lists marriage ministries and organizations. Not all are faith based, but you can scan the list for options of retreats, conferences, and seminars in your area. We don't endorse everyone on the list, so do your homework and check them out thoroughly first. Your pastor should also have several suggestions. Your church or a regional Christian retreat center may also sponsor yearly conferences.

To get the most out of a conference, go the night before and spend time reconnecting in casual conversation, getting some rest, and enjoying a fun activity. Attend the seminar or conference, and then keep your hotel room so that you can "debrief" with a little one-on-one time. In the car on the way home, share the highlights of the time away together, what you learned, and how you'd like to apply the new tools.

A personal private spiritual retreat. Often, Bill and I have pulled away from our daily grind to spend time seeking God. This time might be to search for direction or to prepare for a heavy ministry responsibility or new role. It may simply be to spend time with God, listening to His heart by praying together, reading books and the Bible, and walking and talking through what we sense God saying to us.

Our family has a few favorite conference grounds: Hume Lake, Forest Home Ministries, and Cannon Beach Christian Conference Center are places we go to time after time. Hume Lake has a "Little Brown Church" that sits atop Inspiration Trail and is marked with a rugged cross. We have prayed in the Little Brown Church year after year. We have pictures of Bill and me and our family at all ages and stages in front of that cross. It is a marker, a safe place for our hearts, and a place that consistently provides hope.

At a recent fork in the road that hit our family hard, Bill and I retreated to Hume. Sex in those cabins is always healing and rejuvenating. There is a sweetness in those memories. A sweetness we pray every couple will experience. Sometimes the red-hot monogamy is like a fine chocolate fondue: sweet and rich and slow melting. Investing in your spiritual life can deepen and broaden your intimate connection.

SEXUAL INTIMACY

Finally the one you've all been waiting for! Well, we are going to make you wait just a little longer. This area is so vital, we wanted to give it more time and space and better equip you for a little erotica. So read on, knowing that the best is yet to come. In the next chapter, we'll lay out for you a weekend to remember. A weekend made exclusively, extensively, and specifically to enhance, enrich, and enliven *your* sex life.

GETAWAYS WILL SPARK THE FIRE!

If you take time to get away, you may experience some red-hot monogamy. Like my friend and fellow author Nancy Kennedy, who had a plan to whisk her honey away to do him good.

The Do Him Good Agenda

"She brings him good, not harm
all the days of her life" (Proverbs 31:12).

Let me set the record straight. I didn't mean to do it—any of it. You have to believe me; it was all an accident. I was just trying to, you know, do my husband good, not harm, all the days of my life. Besides, all's well that ends well, right?

It all started the day my friends and I were sitting around, talking. As always, the subject of husbands came up. We started with the usual, "My husband *never* (blah, blah, blah)." "Well, at least yours (yakity yak)." "*Mine* (ya-da, ya-da, ya-da)." You know the routine. After a while, someone changed the subject and began with, "Wouldn't it be fun to do like the books and magazines say and go off on a surprise weekend?" You know, the whole romance bit. Then the excuses started rolling.

Carol went first. "You know I'd do it, but we're still papering the hall bathroom."

Stephanie shrugged her shoulders and pointed to the baby attached to her breast. "I'm still nursing Max and can't leave him yet."

Poor Judy didn't have to say a thing. Last time she and her husband, Don, went away, she had twins nine months later.

All eyes turned to me. I gulped. My mission, should I choose to accept it: Plan a weekend away with Barry.

"No prob," I said. "I can handle it."

A week or so later, I dropped the girls off at Grandma's, packed up the car with a picnic dinner, and in my best madcap, Julia Roberts way, surprised Barry at work, telling him I'm whisking him away for the weekend.

"I don't want to whisk," he said.

"Nonsense," I argued. "We haven't whisked in a long time. Besides, it'll Do You Good."

After a brief discussion (which I won), we whisked off into the sunset. Shortly before six o'clock, we arrived at our first destination: a deserted beach cove where we ate the chicken salad sandwiches I'd packed in my picnic basket that morning. Almost immediately, we discovered why the cove was deserted: the wind seemed to come blasting out of nowhere, whipping sand and bugs into our ears and our eyes and our sandwiches.

One of us wanted to leave, but the other one called him a wimp and insisted that we stay. (I had to. The Do Him Good agenda and all.)

Finally, when one of us couldn't take it any longer, he stumbled up the sand dunes, picking bugs out of his teeth, and hid out in the car, listening to the ball game on the radio. I followed, not too sure he wouldn't make a run for it without me.

After rinsing my sandy teeth with Diet Pepsi and dumping sand out of my shoes, I slid into the passenger seat and flipped off the radio. "Ok, time to turn off the ball game."

"But, but, but..." he said.

We rode along in ball game-less silence while I waited for witty reparte.

I waited a long time.

Finally, Barry cleared his throat as if to speak. My heart fluttered at the hope of a meaningful tête-à-tête. Then: "Why do you have to do that with your teeth?" he asked.

"Do what?"

"That. You always make that clicking noise. Like you're chewing air." He demonstrated.

"I don't do that!" I answered, then pointed my finger at him. "At least I don't eat Styrofoam cups. You can't drink a simple cup of coffee without eating the cup. Most people throw theirs away, you know."

We chewed and clicked for a mile or so until we came to a winding, bumpy road that tossed us at every turn. It wasn't part of the Do Him Good agenda—neither were the waves of nausea and the sharp pains that took our breath away as we were overtaken by an unmistakable bout of black death and/or food poisoning.

Green-faced, Barry steered the car into the parking lot of the first motel he saw and leaned his head on the steering wheel.

"We can't stay here," I said. "This is one of those motels that charge by the hour."

His face changed from green to gray and back to green again. "Do you want to die out here instead?"

A long-haired guy who I thought I recognized from *America's Most Wanted* stopped at our car, belched, and scratched his armpit. Then he flashed a five-toothed grin at me.

That's when I decided, no, I didn't want to die there. We dragged our turning-greener-by-the-minute bodies into the office, signed the register, paid for the next twelve hours and crawled off to Room 132 to...Well, if you've ever had food poisoning, you know what came next. I'll spare you the details.

Sometime during the middle of the night, we died. At least we thought we did. We each saw a bright light, but it turned out to be the red, blinking, neon light that said, MOT L.

As the room spun, we noticed it had been decorated in Early Sleaze motif. You know, clown-hair orange shag carpeting and an avocado green-harvest gold floral bedspread, black velvet paintings of bullfighters hanging cockeyed on peeling, green- and black-flocked, wall-papered walls.

I reached over, turned on the cracked amber glass lamp that was chained to the dresser, then died again for a few hours, rolled together with my snoring husband in the center of the sagging mattress, his elbow in my ribs.

Occasionally, we were partially revived by the sounds of doors opening and closing, heavy footsteps parading up and down the hallway, and a pay phone ringing about every fifteen minutes. Resurrection came around 7 a.m. when a man calling himself Big Buck pounded on the door demanding to see Marie. At 7:01 Buck picked the lock and kicked the door open.

Weak and trembling, we called out from under the covers, "No Marie in here!" Fortunately, Big Buck left as quickly as he came. After he did, we shoved the dresser against the door, showered, put on our same clothes (don't you hate it when you forget something?), and dragged ourselves back to the deserted beach cove to sleep the day away.

Hours later we awoke, sunburned, mosquito-bitten, and scratching, but alive and feeling relatively chipper. One of us announced he was ready to call it quits, but the other one again hinted at someone being a wimp. "Where's your sense of adventure?" I demanded.

"I think I lost it somewhere back at the motel."

I checked my Do Him Good agenda. "Barry, you'll love what comes next: a room overlooking the Atlantic Ocean."

He scratched at the raised, red bumps all down his leg. "I don't want to go," he said.

"It'll Do You Good."

"So will an enema, but I don't want one."

I pulled out my big guns. "It's paid for and non-refundable."

"Let's go."

When we arrived at the door of our beachfront inn, I told Barry to wait outside while I ran inside. Taking a bag of silver confetti out of my purse, I sprinkled it on the bed and around the room. Then I set little candles all around the wooden ledge, which surrounded the bed, lit them to create a romantic glow, and beckoned Barry inside.

Yeah, we smelled. Yeah, we had gunky teeth and bad breath, not to mention sand in our hair and day-old clothes on our bodies. Despite all that, we succumbed to the glow of the flames, although not quite the way that was called for in my Do Him Good agenda.

As we kissed, getting silver confetti in our hair and embedded in our skin, we knocked a candle over and set the blanket ablaze.

"We're on fire!" I gasped.

We flew off the bed. As Barry beat the flames with a pillow, I helped by screaming and pouring a can of soda all over the sheets, the carpet, the bedspread, and everything else. Never before had two lovers produced such sparks!

We spent the rest of the evening laughing as we scrubbed soda stains out of the rug, eating take-out Chinese food, and watching reruns on Nick at Nite—and estimating how much we owed in damages to the room.

"Barry," I said, snuggling up to him as he started to nod off, "you know I only want to do you good, not harm."

"I know," he answered, "and you do, when you're not poisoning me or setting me on fire."

"Really?"

"Really."

I decided to leave it at that, mainly because he began to snore. Eventually, I too drifted off to a peaceful, non-nauseous sleep…As I did, my last thought was of the next day's Do Him Good plan: Cancel Do Him Good bungee-jumping; listen to ball game on the way home.[2]

Hands-on Homework

*E*ach of you create an invitation to one of the types of getaways below. (Note: the sexual intimacy getaway isn't on the list; that's the hands-on homework for chapter 5.)

- Social
- Financial
- Recreational
- Vocational
- Parental
- Emotional
- Spiritual

Even if the getaway is for a serious issue, such as vocation or finances, try to be creative in the invitation. Remember, the result of any of these getaways is to work out issues ahead of time so you can create deeper, stronger, and richer intimate bonds that then lead to red-hot monogamy more naturally. For a vocational getaway, a wife might place something small and lacy in her mate's briefcase with her invitation. For a financial getaway, take a check and write out "To my loving, red-hot honey." Amount: 100 kisses and no interruptions. Sign it "Your (insert your nickname.)"

After you each give your invitations, decide when to schedule them both sometime over the next year.

Red-Hot ROMANCE IDEAS

76. Make a trail of rose petals that lead from the front door through the house to your bedroom (or another room) you have prepared exclusively for some red-hot monogamy.

77. Spend the night in heaven. Rent a dry ice machine from a theater company to form a cloud around your bed.

78. Plant a tree in a park (some parks offer this program). Go back year after year for a picnic under that same tree.

79. Have a star named for your mate, and then take him or her out stargazing on a hillside in some secluded spot. (If it is secluded enough, you might get a little red-hot monogamy.)

80. Give your mate a day off. Select a day he or she has set aside to do a huge task (paint the house, clean the house, clean the rain gutters) and then arrange for someone else to accomplish that chore while you send your mate to the spa for the morning or whisk him or her to a resort with you for 24 hours.

81. Leave a mint on the pillow. Put your own fortune in a fortune cookie. Bake a message into a cupcake or cookie. Write a message in icing on a mega cookie or cake top.

82. Engrave it. Make a key chain with a heart engraved with your wedding date or the date you first met. Engrave a clock that says "I will always make time for you." Engrave a pen or pen box with "Not enough words to say how

much I love you." Engrave his or her house key with "The key to my heart."

83. Buy some temporary tattoos and tattoo each other in a not-so-public place on your bodies. Or temporarily tattoo yourself and ask your mate to find where you placed it.

84. Do something on a date that you rarely do. Go to the zoo. Go to the park and feed the ducks. Go to the thrift shop and buy something outrageous. Skinny-dip in your backyard pool when the kids aren't home.

85. Do something active. Take a walk, fly a kite, go kayaking, skiing, bicycling, swimming, sailing, or ice or roller skating. Endorphins make you happy, and happy lovers enjoy red-hot monogamy! If you become more active, you'll get in shape and maybe make love with the lights ON for a change.

86. Take a ballroom dance class or private dance lessons.

87. Learn to two-step or swing dance. (Dancing is like foreplay to most women.)

88. Get out a map or book on hiking trails and national parks. See if you can locate a romantic secluded lake or a waterfall pool. (What you do there is your business.)

89. Get all dressed up and head to the upscale shops of your community. Just window-shop and then eat at someplace very nice. If money is tight, order an appetizer.

90. Do a theme date. Eat pasta or pizza with Italian music playing. Have a Mexican fiesta meal and wear a hand-embroidered dress partly unlaced to dinner with a mariachi band playing as he finishes unlacing it. Eat French cuisine and afterward practice your French kissing.

91. Eat at the airport. (Really, some have nice food!) Dream about places around the world you'd like to travel together.

92. Model for each other while you take turns sketching or taking photos.

93. Have a Sunday afternoon pajama party. Set aside Sunday afternoon for a nap. (Okay, you don't have to sleep.)

94. Practice pickup lines. Make a game of it anytime you are meeting your mate. Walk up to your already seated spouse and try some new line on him or her as if you were meeting for the very first time.

95. Have coffee at a bookstore and be intellectual. Discuss deep, philosophical issues or classic works of literature. It is even more fun if you have no idea what you are talking about. For one night pretend you are a brain surgeon or the scientist who discovered DNA.

96. Invite your mate to a "your love has lifted me higher" date. Take him or her up in a hot air balloon, to a restaurant that rotates on top a skyscraper, or for a private plane ride.

97. Watch the sunset or sunrise. Slow down your pace by enjoying some food or drink at one of these two daily moments. Try to find the most romantic place in your town or neighborhood to watch the sun set and rise.

98. Go to a train station or airport and decide right there, spontaneously where to travel for a few days. For an extra spark of spontaneity, bring only your tooth brush and get anything you need along the way. You can also take a car trip this way. Use a die: If you roll a 1, head north; 2 means

south; 3, west; 4, east. Drive till you are hungry or tired or spot some fun thing to do.

99. Have a cultural date. Stroll through an art gallery, find a street artisan fair, attend a play or opera.

100. Spread lotion or oil onto one another and then have sex on a new fresh shower curtain that has been spread on your bed for a grown-up version of Slip 'n Slide.

5

Come on, Baby, Light My Fire, Part 1

IDEAS TO FAN THE FLAME

We know our writer friend Deb definitely has red-hot monogramy going on because she shared this recent erotic escapade with us in an e-mail:

On a romantic weekend in Carmel, my husband treated me to a suite overlooking the ocean at the Carmel Highlands Inn. The room was as exquisite as the view, with a fireplace, nice comfy chairs, and even a bottle of champagne from the manager.

We'd heard about the inn from a friend in L.A. who told us that when he and his wife were there, they sipped the champagne, lit the fire, admired the view, and then lit another fire between themselves. As things were getting hotter, the smoke alarm went off...they were so embarrassed.

Needless to say, history repeated itself. We admired the view, lit a fire in the fireplace...and kindled flames between us...and the smoke alarm went off. When we called the front desk to say there was no fire, a very bored young man sighed. "Never mind, lady. It happens all the time."

We think this is a great goal—sex so hot that it sets off the fire alarm! And wouldn't it be great if those who know you best said, "It happens all the time"?

TRAITS OF A RED-HOT LOVER

In the study guide for our book *Men Are Like Waffles—Women Are Like Spaghetti,* we point out that "overall, the best way to a better marriage is to become a better partner. The best way to become a better partner is to become a better person." In other words, if you want to have a great sex life, you need to make it your goal to become a great lover.

Recently Dr. Tim LaHaye and his wife, Beverly, authors of *The Act of Marriage After 40,* reminded us that the French have a saying: "There is no such thing as a frigid woman, only inept men."[1] Now, don't be too harsh on the men. For too long we women have used PMS, headaches, the kids, work, and the lint in the dryer (or whatever other creative excuse we can come up with) for not investing in a more active sexual life.

We all long for the kind of red-hot monogamy that sets off fireworks, but that kind of intimate life does not happen by accident. We must each be willing to prepare ourselves, our minds, and our attitudes. The experience of orgasm can be enjoyed physically on a regular basis if you cultivate the experience in your heart and your mind first. You are much more likely to fully enjoy being intimate if you have anticipated it in your mind and longed for it in your heart. To help you in this preparation process, we have come up with an acrostic that displays the traits of a lover who can really set a spouse ablaze with excitement and passion. A red-hot lover is:

Others centered
Risk taker
God focused
Attentive
Self-aware
Mature

Yep. We thought if we spelled out "orgasm," you might remember the acrostic and what each letter stands for, even in the heat of passion.

Others Centered

We are not naive enough to think that any of you will experience orgasm every time you have sex, but that is not really the goal. The goal of love is to help your spouse become the very best person he or she can be. When this goal includes being a lover who can bring your partner to orgasm, your entire relationship will be better. In the *Life Enrich* video series on sexuality, the American Association of Christian Counselors includes a section on "Passionate Intimacy." Four Christian sex therapists gave their advice on what produces passionate sex. Below is a paraphrased summary:

- A good, fulfilling sex life is more than learning skills or techniques...it is more than just getting our spouse to see sex from our viewpoint.

- Couples too often get into a routine; he touches me this way, I respond that way...but if we seek to connect emotionally and not just chase the orgasm, orgasms will happen as an outgrowth of the connectedness.

- Not only are we becoming naked physically—but deeply connected sex is looking into each other's hearts and souls. Great sex is exposing each other.

- Take time to drink in each other fully clothed and you'll see the benefit when you undress.

In the Old Testament, the term most often used for the act of intercourse is translated in our English Bibles as "to lay with." This does not mean they laid down and took a nap. No, it is the common term for having sex. But the full meaning of this unique Hebrew word is "to know." A more complete definition includes, "to be made known; to be revealed; to be perceived; to be instructed; to be taught to be known."[2] True passion, the kind that produces red-hot monogamy, is the quest to know and be known by your spouse. It is vulnerability. It is seeking to make an emotionally safe environment so your mate can feel free to unveil his or her real self, his or her innermost thoughts, feelings, and emotions. To unleash passion, your spouse needs to feel loved and cared for by you. He or she needs to sense it is safe to trust you with his or her heart and emotions. Your spouse must be able to let his or her guard down or (especially for women) orgasm will never happen. To experience orgasm, the sexual encounter needs to be a place of freedom and release.

To accomplish this goal, think of your role as a sexual partner like that of a spotter. I (Pam) was, at one time, a competitive gymnast. When learning dangerous new tricks, we always had a coach or fellow teammate "spot" us. They kept their full attention on me and their hands were ready to catch me, especially at strategic moments, and their whole job was to keep me from falling. They were my safety net.

To make your spouse feel comfortable enough to really trust you sexually and be vulnerable enough to experience freedom, you need to communicate that same level of tender, loving care.

You need to be the net under their heart and soul. To accomplish this goal, sex can't be all about you, all about your needs, or all about your fulfillment. For sex to be mutually satisfying and reach the level of "red-hot," both lovers have to take their eyes off themselves and their own pleasure to focus on the pleasure of the other. If both the husband and the wife are seeking to please the other, pleasure will happen for both of them. Sometimes the pleasure doesn't happen at the same, simultaneous moment, and that's okay because you are making a lifetime investment. At other times, mutual orgasm will be God's gift to you because He will smile down and give that kind of wonderful sense of timing.

A little FYI to women: Sexual release appears to be much simpler for men than it is for us. God has naturally programmed into the male anatomy the ability to ejaculate pretty much every time. It may not always happen as a man gets older, but for the most part, ejaculation is not a problem. This is not the only goal a man has for sex, however. He also longs to feel emotionally safe around you, but he may not talk about it or even be able to express it to you. He looks to sex not just for physical release (not to downplay the fact that he completely and readily enjoys that part), but he also wants sex to make him feel emotionally stronger, to give him the gift of feeling on top of the world and invincible. An emotionally safe environment will also help him feel vulnerable enough to risk trying different ways and techniques to please you. So, you are your own best friend when you seek to also meet the emotional need in your husband. Dr. Ed Wheat, author of *Intended for Pleasure*, once said, "Every sexual union should be a contest to see which partner can out please the other."

Take a moment to ask your spouse, sometime this week, what makes him or her feel emotionally and sexually comfortable with you:

- What do I say or do outside the bedroom that makes you feel you can trust me?

- What do I say or do outside the bedroom that makes you feel comfortable around me?

- What things do I say or do while we make love that make you feel comfortable, free, secure, and valued?

- Specifically, what things (touches, words, positions, techniques) do I do in bed that help you come to climax? Which are your favorites?

Light at the End of the Tunnel

One way to develop a high sexual comfort level is to have at least one night or time per week that you *know* you two will have sex. Some ask, "Schedule sex? I thought it was supposed to be spontaneous." We have found that if you have a regular time each week that you both know sex will happen, then it is like laying a foundation for sex in your relationship, and a lot can be built on a strong foundation. Jill Savage, the author of *Is There Sex After Kids?* gives some positive reasons for scheduling a weekly sex date:

Scheduling Sex Eliminates "The Ask"

In most marriages, one partner possesses a higher desire than the other and requests sex more often, while their partner rarely asks for physical intimacy. For the spouse with a higher desire, the fear of rejection often sets in. One becomes weary of having to ask, or even beg, for sex on a regular basis.

When a couple can agree upon a basic schedule for sex in marriage, it takes the guesswork out. While this still leaves room for occasional spontaneity, it reassures the higher-sex-drive partner that it will happen and not only that—they know when! Usually the schedule is less often than the partner with a higher desire would want and more frequently than the partner with a lesser desire may want. Instead, it's meeting on middle ground.

Scheduling Sex Increases Desire

For the partner with a diminished desire, scheduling sex engages the brain because it's the largest sex organ in the human body. The brain needs to be clued to prepare the body for a sexual response. Most people who have a lower sexual drive simply don't think about sex very often. Scheduling sex jump-starts this process.

Once sex is on the calendar, it provides a mental reminder to think about sex, prepares us mentally for being together physically, and primes us to do whatever it takes to "get in the mood."

When I complained to a friend about having trouble getting in the mood, she said, "Jill, are you trying to go from making meatloaf to making love in thirty seconds flat? You can't do that. You have to have a strategy for going from point A to point B."

Rarely does the partner with an increased desire need to get "in the mood." In contrast, the partner with a lesser desire may need to work at it. When sex is on the calendar though, it serves as a prompt to set strategies in motion. Scheduling sex reminds spouses that they are working together toward the goal of intimacy, valuing their appointed rendezvous, and doing whatever it takes to make it happen.

Scheduling Sex Increases Anticipation

When lovemaking is kept on the front burner, it builds anticipation. Both husband and wife begin to intentionally anticipate and prepare for their marital recreation.

Have you ever thought of sex as recreation? It is! God gave us the gift of sex as a form of recreation in our marriage. It's our own private playground where God intends for us to enjoy physical pleasure.

When sex is on the schedule, we enjoy planning our time together because we both hold the same goal. We can even become a lifelong learner of giving pleasure to one another. Keeping a couple of Christian sexual technique books on the shelf may also develop us into a connoisseur of giving physical pleasure to our spouse, and it builds anticipation as you plan and think about the next time you will be together.

Scheduling Sex Allows For Prime-Time Planning

He prefers nighttime when he can be romantic. She prefers daytime when she's not so tired. They decide that twice a week lovemaking is on their calendar—Tuesday at noon (he comes home for lunch and she arranges a sitter for the kids) and Friday at night (after a warm bath and an evening of watching a movie together or going out on a date). This schedule worked well for one couple that we mentored through a challenging season in their marriage.

Most couples not only differ in their desires concerning frequency of sex, but also in the atmosphere that is conducive to sex. Some struggle with making love anytime children are in the vicinity. Others prefer a certain time of the day. When you put your lovemaking on the calendar, you can work to accommodate those likes/dislikes to meet the needs of both.

Scheduling Sex Helps Couples Prepare Physically

I often tease my husband that once we got on a lovemaking schedule, it sure took the pressure off to shave my legs every day! On a serious side, there's value in preparing yourself physically to make love to your mate. A hot bath or shower, a freshly shaved body, and some great-smelling body lotion often relaxes us for physical intimacy. It also builds anticipation as you prepare to be with your spouse.

If weariness keeps you from being excited about sex, an early evening nap may be just the key if lovemaking is on the agenda that night. Since some of the guesswork is out of the mix, we can prepare not only mentally, but physically for our time together.

Scheduling Sex Builds Trust in a Marriage

If we're going to commit to lovemaking on a regular basis, we need to honor our word and agreement. When we honor our word, it builds trust and deepens intimacy in our relationship. On the rare occasion that something circumvents your regular lovemaking schedule, spouses need to communicate their value for sexual intimacy so that alternate plans are made to meet the physical and emotional needs within your marriage. This is the key to successfully calendaring your lovemaking…Spontaneous sex may have its place in life, but scheduling sex always has its place on our calendar![3]

Attitude Adjustment

Sometimes our schedule isn't the only thing that needs adjusting; our attitude may need adjusting too. Often we come to the sexual encounter wanting our needs to be the first on the docket. However, a pleasant surprise to us is that when we make the goal of sex to emotionally connect with our mate and give him or her pleasure, the love boomerangs back around, and we discover something new that is fun or fulfilling to us as well. I think God smiles on us when we seek to have an attitude adjustment. Instead of praying, "Lord, change my mate," pray, "Lord, change me." You will see some incredible results from that prayer. My (Pam's) friend Marita Littauer, author of *Love Extravagantly*, shared this story with me:

> My husband doesn't like it when I travel. Traveling has been a part of my life, though, for all my adult years.

When I met Chuck, I was teaching seminars all over the country and still am. You'd think he'd be used to it after twenty years of marriage. Instead, he likes it less and less.

While on the plane ride home from seminars, I often enjoy escaping into a romance novel. As I read, I picture Chuck meeting me at the airport terminal with roses in his hand, or at least dropping what he's doing when I walk in the door at home. Then he hugs me and kisses me and confirms how much he's missed me. Not.

In reality, the plane lands. I deplane and walk alone through the terminal, get my baggage, and go to my car. I wait in line to pay for my parking and drive home. Because I like to get home from a trip as soon as possible, I frequently arrive late at night rather than the next day. So Chuck is often asleep. I tiptoe in, drop my bags, and undress in the dark. I crawl into bed beside him, and he wiggles his foot against my leg to welcome me home. Hardly the romance-novel scene I'd painted in my mind.

One year, my trip had me scheduled to arrive home on the day of our anniversary. It was our sixteenth, and I really wanted that romance-novel scene I'd so often dreamed about.

I'd arranged to have flowers sent to his office with a card that said "Happy Anniversary! Hurry home after work!" (The flowers would be delivered in the morning in case he forgot what day it was, and they'd remind him to do whatever he needed to do.) I'd also planned to arrive home before he got off work, so I'd have time to shop for the ingredients to make a lovely dinner.

When I got home, I headed straight for the kitchen, did the dinner prep work, and put it all aside. When I went into the bedroom, I found something small and black hanging on our four-poster bed with an anniversary card. (He hadn't forgotten after all.) After relaxing in a bubble bath, I put on my present and lit some candles in the bedroom. Next, I put something bubbly in a silver bucket, and placed it, along with two crystal flutes, next to the bed. When it was nearly time for him to come home, I crawled up on the bed and read my romance novel—and waited. The dogs barked and I heard his car door. I tucked the romance novel away and arranged myself artfully across the bed.

From the results of my efforts, I could now write a romance novel of my own! He was excited to see me, glad I'd come home. While the night left me breathless, I thought it through in the morning. That was the reaction I'd like every time I get home!

Romans 12:18 tells me that it's my job to do the changing, not to change him. What could I change that would bring about the desired effect? First, I could change my schedule so I came home before he did, instead of after he was asleep. I could fix a special dinner and bring on the bubbly. I could put on one of the many "little somethings" he's given me over the years that I know he likes, and I can place myself across the bed as if in a lingerie catalog. Yes, I could do that.

And my next trip, I did just that. It worked again—even without the special day and without the flowers. My next trip, I tried it again, and it worked again. I'd created an attitude adjustment.

While Chuck is still not crazy about my traveling, he sure loves my coming home! But without travel, would I be putting forth the homecoming effort? Perhaps not. Perhaps being apart makes being together that much more exciting. Perhaps travel isn't so bad after all.[4]

A Risk Taker

To be a red-hot lover, one who can both experience orgasm and give that same rush to your mate, you have to be willing to take risks in bed. (Or anyplace else you might want to enjoy sex. Try some new places. After all, you are a risk taker, right?)

There are a couple attitudes you will need in order to be a risk taker in romance and as a sex partner.

You don't have to be thin or young to enjoy red-hot monogamy. Studies say that the hottest sex is experienced among those who have been happily married for some time. We don't know about you, but as you look around at all your middle-aged friends, how many hard bodies do you see? We see very few "specimens," but there are plenty of love handles in the crowd. You know what? For the most part we could all shed a few pounds and probably live a bit longer. We also noticed that not one of us looks like a runway model or professional athlete. Actually, most of us are just plain—average! But we all experience red-hot monogamy on a regular basis. Why? We have gotten over ourselves. We all have (1) accepted our bodies, and (2) taken our eyes off ourselves so we can focus on our spouses.

Your most vital sex organ, the most erogenous zone of your body, is your brain. If you decide you will be a red-hot lover, you will become a red-hot lover. Let's take a look at our sample couple, Sol and Sunny.

In chapter 4 of the Song of Songs, the two lovers are captivated with one another. Check out Sol's words to his bride:

> How beautiful you are, my darling! Oh, how beautiful! Your eyes behind your veil are doves. Your hair is like a flock of goats descending from Mount Gilead. Your teeth are like a flock of sheep just shorn, coming up from the washing. Each has its twin; not one of them is alone. Your lips are like a scarlet ribbon; your mouth is lovely. Your temples behind your veil are

like the halves of a pomegranate. Your neck is like the tower of David, built with elegance; on it hang a thousand shields, all of them shields of warriors. Your two breasts are like two fawns, like twin fawns of a gazelle that browse among the lilies (Song of Songs 4:1-5).

And he goes on like this for ten more verses.

In response to Sol's praise, Sunny enthusiastically welcomes the impending sexual encounter:

Awake, north wind, and come, south wind! Blow on my garden, that its fragrance may spread abroad. Let my lover come into his garden and taste its choice fruits (Song of Songs 4:16).

You need to keep a sense of humor to maintain your risk-taker mind-set. We love a story a couple sent to us after one of our seminars. The husband (we'll call him "Will"), is writing this e-mail :

I believe the Lord definitely has a sense of humor when it comes to sex in marriage. My wife and I went to the mountains eight years ago for our "one-year anniversary fling." We rented a little cabin way up in the woods, and it happened to have a hot tub. (Strategic planning on my part.)

We arrived on a Friday and settled in for the night, so the festivities didn't get to really take place until the next morning. My wife surprised me by suggesting a fling in the hot tub out on the back porch. She informed me that this would be a no-clothes event, and that the only requirement was that she gets to go first and get settled in before I arrived. I told her "NO PROBLEM!" She went in first and needless to say, I followed soon. With nothing but my starched white boxers on, I took off after her. (The boxers will play an important role in this story very soon.)

We had some married fun in the hot tub for a while, and my wife asked me to run in and get her a towel. I obliged and went across the porch to go back into the house. The only problem was that the doors were like hotel rooms, and they electronically locked behind you when you exited. NO KEY! I told her to hang tight. I ran to the side door to see if it was open. No luck! I looked left and right first and then streaked to the front of the house to see if we had left the front door open. Still no luck.

I ran back to the porch and informed her that we had a slight problem. Between the two of us, all that was left was a wet pair of boxers. I put them on and started walking down the mountain to knock on the neighbor's door to humbly ask them to call the front cabin office for us so we could get another key. Everyone had already left for the morning, so off I went to the next house. No one was home there, either. This went on door to door down the mountain. (Let me paint the picture. The road was paved with big pieces of gravel, so I walked like a 90-year-old man barefooted on the side of the road, and the only thing whiter than my wet boxers was my big belly hanging over them and the wide tail that they tried to cover.)

After 30 minutes of walking, an old man in a pickup saw me. He laughed his head off and then took me back to my cabin. He was nice enough to run and get us a key. When we arrived, my wife looked like a lobster (one hour in the hot tub will do that to a girl!). Needless to say, it was a day that I, my wife, and the little old man in the mountains will never forget.

Please use this story whenever needed to tell others how much fun it can be when everything seems to go wrong. Situations like these only bring you closer. Of all of our encounters together, this one is the one that we return to every now and then for a good laugh.

If "Will" and his very pink wife can overcome this amazing love mishap and go on to experience red-hot monogamy (and she really was "red and hot"), then we all can get a grip and not take our mistakes or uncomfortable sexual situations too seriously. We should just regroup and go on.

Seriously, think back to some of the things and positions and places you have tried. Think about some of the crazy positions you can end up being in during the throes of passion. It is like a pretzel out of control sometimes. When we find ourselves being not so smooth, we just whisper, "Sorry. Let me shift a bit here." Or if your mate is trying something that is just not at all doing it for you or is flat out painful, then gently give a change-of-course suggestion, such as, "Thanks, sweetie, but can you (go a little lower, try a little slower)." Simply remind him or her of something you really love, or shift gears and move to something he or she really loves. Regrouping with a smile and a lot of sensitive tact is an attractive quality in a lover.

One woman shared with me (Pam) at a conference after a session on sex in marriage. "I suggested that we pull off onto a secluded dirt road one night coming home from church. My husband about fainted when I unbuckled his seat belt and climbed on to his lap facing him. I found out that the enjoyment and pleasure of red-hot monogamy (as you call it), can outweigh the pain induced by a steering wheel in the back. I would definitely risk sex in the car again, but this time I might suggest the backseat."

Turn Up the Passion Volume

When the truth is turned up in your mind, you are freed to be the confident lover God designed you to be. For example, I (Pam) would like to give a word of advice and encouragement to the ladies reading this book. Please work on your self-consciousness and inhibitions. The sexual relationship you have is with *your husband.* Try to be open to a few new ideas or come up with a few new plans or places yourself. Your husband, like all men, lives for adventure, so if you are fulfilling that need in his life, he will be happier, easier to live with, more generous, and more motivated to please you. You will do your relationship a favor if you ask yourself, "How can I develop enough confidence to be willing to risk?"

In my own life, I realized the Bible said, "The truth will set you free." If I turn up the truth, then I am free to be the woman God designed me to be. So I recite the truth to myself. "Lord, You say I am fearfully and wonderfully made. I accept my body as wonderful." (Or, if it is a PMS day, "Lord, help me accept by faith that my body is wonderful, or just have Bill see my body as wonderful. That's a cool miracle too.") "God, You say I am Bill's helpmate and that every good gift comes down from You, Father, so I believe I am a gift from You to Bill to help him succeed in all areas of life, even in his sexuality." I learned I had more control over my emotional state than I thought. I decided to believe God's truth that I am beautiful. I am capable. I am God's gift to Bill. So with God's help I can surprise Bill and fulfill him. And with the affirmations comes the fruit, so much so that I can get a little bold. "Lord, with Your turning up the truth, I think I can gain the ability to fly Bill to the moon in raptured ecstasy!" (It's a little over the top, I know, but God's pep talk does more for a woman than the Little Engine mantra, "I think I can, I think I can, I think I can..." God takes you to the last page of the book, "I know I can, I know I can, I know I can..." do all things (even provide awesome red-hot monogamy) through Christ who strengthens me (Philippians 4:13 NKJV).

The outcome of camping on the truth is amazing. I was able to experiment with a few new ideas and risk a little. In being more daring, I found we both enjoyed sex more. If I simply allow myself to be fully overcome with my precious feelings for Bill, risk taking becomes natural. He loves it when I unexpectedly give him a passionate kiss when he was expecting a simple quick kiss goodbye or hello. He sure smiles when I grab him by his suit lapel and whisper, "I have a minute—do you?" He definitely appreciated it when I have said, while driving, "Pull over, right here, right now—or get me home fast!" He values the new outfits (or lack thereof), the new ideas, the new places, the new plans. He appreciates that I have been thinking of him enough to come up with anything new at all because what that says is, "You are more important than my work, the kids' schedule, the house, or my agenda."

God Focused

Remember the "sexperts" from the *Life Enrich* videos mentioned in the last chapter? One member of the team got everyone else's attention when he said, "Good sex is about becoming a mature person—getting rid of selfishness and developing Christlikeness." We couldn't agree more.

So a question that will help all of us become red-hot lovers is, "What is Christlikeness and how does that look in a sexual relationship, especially considering that Jesus never had sex?" While Christ didn't experience sex firsthand, He did create it. At the time of creation, God came up with the great idea of sex, so we think Christ definitely has some valid opinions on the topic.

The place to begin is with Jesus' character. Philippians 2:4-8 says: "Each of you should look not only to your own interests, but also to the interests of others. Your attitude should be the same as that of Christ Jesus: Who, being in very nature God, did not consider equality with God something to be grasped, but made himself nothing, taking the very nature of a servant…he humbled himself."

Red-hot lovers are humble and God focused. One day at lunch, a couple friends and I (Pam) talked about what makes a great husband. We all were Christian speakers and leaders. After a very brief conversation about how supportive and hardworking for the mission and vision our spouses were, and how they pitched in at deadline time and tackled hard technical problems for us, one woman said, "My husband takes that attitude with him into the bedroom. Our lovemaking is often all about me, and he looks for ways to thrill me and please me." Then, one by one, the rest of us said, "Me too. Sometimes I just can't believe how great he can make me feel!" and "I know, my husband has that trait too!" I then began to hum the 1950s tune, "You Send Me." We all decided we were indeed extremely fortunate. I am pretty sure I have never heard, "Have an Amazing Husband Lover" as a bullet point for creating a successful speaking ministry at any writers' and speakers' conferences, but we have a sneaking suspicion if more leaders were vulnerable about their own love lives, we might see a pattern emerge.

I can always tell on Sunday if Bill enjoyed having a "hot time in the ol' town" with me the night before. He speaks with more confidence, clarity, power, and authority, and he seems to enjoy his leadership role more. I smile inside knowingly when people come up to me and say, "Wow, Bill was really incredible today!" (Once, Bill was standing near me when a parishioner complimented him with those words. After they left, he bent down and whispered, "It was because you were incredible last night.")

To Say Yes Is a Godly Thing

We also remember the church that brought Bill and me in to speak because I had such a healthy attitude about sexuality. One of the leading women Bible study teachers had been teaching for years (unbeknownst to the pastor) that if you are truly spiritual, you don't need sex anymore. The pastor couldn't figure out why all his deacons and elders were so grumpy, disinterested, and short-tempered until one day, in a fit of frustration in an elder meeting, one elder said, "Maybe I wouldn't be so short-tempered if I ever got sex at home. It's been years, Pastor!" Most of the other leaders nodded in agreement, and through discussion they traced the problem back to the unscriptural teaching that had infiltrated the church. I think we received more thank-you notes from that congregation after we taught there than pretty much any place else we have spoken (from husbands *and* wives).

It seems they had simply forgotten verses such as 1 Corinthians 7:5: "Do not *deprive* each other except by mutual consent and for a time, so that you may devote yourselves to prayer. Then come together again so that Satan will not tempt you because of your lack of self-control" (emphasis added).

Bill and I have made it a goal to not say no. That doesn't mean we never beg off or ask for a rain check, but we try not to.

> Since there is so much immorality, each man should have his own wife, and each woman her own husband. The husband should fulfill his marital duty to his wife, and likewise the wife to her husband. The wife's body does not belong to her alone but also to her husband. In the same way, the husband's body does not belong to him alone but also to his wife (1 Corinthians 7:2-4).

And in The Message, the instruction is even clearer:

> It's good for a man to have a wife, and for a woman to have a husband. Sexual drives are strong, but marriage is strong enough to contain them and provide for a balanced and fulfilling sexual life in a world of sexual disorder. The marriage bed must be a place of mutuality—the husband seeking to satisfy his wife, the wife seeking to satisfy her husband. Marriage is not a place to "stand up for your rights." Marriage is a decision to serve the other, whether in bed or out. Abstaining from sex is permissible for a period of time if you both agree to it, and if it's for the purposes of prayer and fasting—but only for such times. Then

come back together again. Satan has an ingenious way
of tempting us when we least expect it. I'm not, understand, commanding these periods of abstinence—only
providing my best counsel if you should choose them
(1 Corinthians 7:2-6).

It is truly spiritual to be truly sexual (within the context of
marriage). And it is most spiritual to be in line with God's advice,
and God advises we say yes to our spouse (unless *both* of you
decide otherwise for a short period of time).

We consider ourselves so fortunate to have received this great
advice as newlyweds. Even before we married, I (Pam) spent the
summer at the Institute of Biblical Studies sponsored by Campus
Crusade for Christ, where I took a four-week course on Christian Love and Marriage taught by FamilyLife founder Dennis
Rainey. In seminary we had many authors in the area as professors: Norm Wright, Jim and Sally Conway, Rex Johnson, and
others. Then we had the good fortune of attending a Marriage
Encounter weekend. We also read good books that were recom-
mended to us, including *Intended for Pleasure* by Dr. Ed Wheat
and his wife, Gaye, and *The Act of Marriage* by Dr. Tim LaHaye
and his wife, Beverly. During the first few years of marriage we
came across *Solomon on Sex* by Joseph Dillow, which is a devotional commentary on the book of Song of Songs in the Bible.
And like many couples, we have benefited from the teachings
of Gary Smalley. All of these resources freed us to see that sex
is definitely a spiritual act. To be married and truly obedient to
Christ, you must take seriously the admonition: Your body is not
your own, but your spouse's.

I (Pam) remember praying about this command one day. My
prayer went something like, *Lord, You know I absolutely love sex
with Bill. He is so awesome. You also know I struggle with migraines. I want to say yes to Bill as much as possible, but I really do*

have to sometimes say, "Not tonight, I have a headache." Can You solve this for me, God?

Shortly after that prayer, I had a doctor's appointment for my migraines. As I sat in the waiting room, I read a medical magazine with a small article in it that said sex opens up the blood vessels, so it actually lessens the pain for migraines. I have since changed my response. Now it is, "Honey, yes tonight. I have a headache." It is much more fun to reach for Bill when I feel a headache coming on instead of just reaching for a bottle of pain reliever.

What Does Love Look Like?

In the book of 1 John we are told, "God is love" (1 John 4:8,16). So the very essence and character we see in Christ should be our model for human relationships. The more we seek to be like Christ, the more loving we will naturally become. Much is gained when we look at Christ's priorities and values and how He defines love:

> Love is patient, love is kind. It does not envy, it does not boast, it is not proud. It is not rude, it is not self-seeking, it is not easily angered, it keeps no record of wrongs. Love does not delight in evil but rejoices with the truth. It always protects, always trusts, always hopes, always perseveres. Love never fails (1 Corinthians 13:4-8).

> The fruit of the Spirit is love, joy, peace, patience, kindness, goodness, faithfulness, gentleness and self-control (Galatians 5:22-23).

> Blessed are the poor in spirit, for theirs is the kingdom of heaven. Blessed are those who mourn, for they will be comforted. Blessed are the meek, for they will inherit the earth. Blessed are those who hunger and thirst for righteousness, for they will be filled. Blessed are the merciful, for they will be shown mercy. Blessed

are the pure in heart, for they will see God. Blessed
are the peacemakers, for they will be called sons of
God. Blessed are those who are persecuted because
of righteousness, for theirs is the kingdom of heaven.
Blessed are you when people insult you, persecute you
and falsely say all kinds of evil against you because of
me. Rejoice and be glad, because great is your reward
in heaven, for in the same way they persecuted the
prophets who were before you (Matthew 5:3-12).

Therefore, as God's chosen people, holy and dearly
loved, clothe yourselves with compassion, kindness,
humility, gentleness and patience. Bear with each other
and forgive whatever grievances you may have against
one another. Forgive as the Lord forgave you. And over
all these virtues put on love, which binds them all together in perfect unity (Colossians 3:12-14).

All these verses explain how God thinks people should treat
one another. When I turn up the truth in my heart and soul,
then I remember how to treat my mate in a way that produces
a positive result, and the outcome is pure pleasure and passion.
Righteous living produces righteous red-hot monogamy.

We'll pick up in the next chapter even more red-hot traits that
can produce sizzling sex.

Hands-on Homework

*I*f being others centered is a key to unlocking passion and unzipping sexual opportunities, then schedule some time this week to sit in the hot tub, a bubble bath, or in front of the fireplace together and answer some questions that will give you more insights into your mate's heart:

> *You are a work of art:*
> > *When I first saw you, I thought…*
> > *What were you thinking?*
>
> *You are a puzzle:*
> > *The thing I still can't figure out about you is…*
> > *Does something still puzzle you about me?*
>
> *You are in my dreams:*
> > *My favorite dream with you in it was…*
> > *What do you dream that we might do someday?*
>
> *You make my heart sing:*
> > *The song that most reminds me of you is…*
> > *What words would you love to hear me sing to you?*
>
> *You keep me up at night:*
> > *I worry most about you when…*
> > *What makes you worry?*
>
> *You are the air I breathe:*
> > *I want to touch you sexually _____ times a (day/week),*
> > *and I like to show it by_____.*
> > *How will I know when you want to touch me?*

You light my fire:
   I feel sexual sensation that makes me want you when...
   What gives you those feelings?

You are my inspiration:
   After making love with you, I feel as though I could...
   How does red-hot monogamy make you feel?

You make my head spin:
   I feel delirious with exhilaration when you...
   What do I (do, say, touch) that makes your heart pound
   with excitement?

You light up the room:
   If people only know how well you _____ ,
   you'd be given a World's Best Red-Hot Lover award.
   What do I (say/do) that brightens your life?

Red-Hot
ROMANCE IDEAS

101. Rent bicycles with baskets on the handlebars and bike to the bank of a creek, lake, or river. Fill the baskets with the makings of a Parisian picnic: Perrier water, French bread, Brie, and a blanket.

102. Camp in the living room. (You will have to farm the kids out for an overnighter at a friend's.)

103. Have sex in all the rooms of your home. Make it your goal to "christen" every room in the house with a sexual encounter. (Bonus points for the kitchen and garage.)

104. Stock up on favorite arousal smells. Each of you make a list of fragrances you love: fresh-baked brownies to plumeria to a certain perfume or cologne. Have them all around so you can scent the air, signaling your spouse that you are in the mood.

105. Give each other $10 and a 20-minute limit to stop by a Wal-Mart, Kmart, or Target to buy something that will make sex fun. Share the surprise when you both get home to your bedroom.

106. Get a piece of fabric to use for a veil and practice a belly dance for him as he takes in the wonderful sight of you. Be sure to drape the veil over and around him at key moments. See if he can make it even through one Middle Eastern song before he is up and out of the chair...

107. Turn your master bath into a luxury spa. Have plenty of spa amenities available, and create a unique menu of available services you are offering to your spouse.

108. Revive Rome! Wrap yourself and your spouse in a toga (a bed sheet will make a nice one). Toss all kinds of pillows on the floor and then recline as you drop grapes into each other's mouths.

109. Try a new sexual position.

110. Draw a masterpiece—with body paint on your mate.

111. Reread the section on designing your boudoir in chapter 2 and head to the store for some new items for your room. Test your new digs by seeing what the view is from both lying or sitting on the bed and making love on the floor, or check the scene from the lovemaking session on the vanity counter.

112. Try making love in your own backyard. You might have to do a little prep work to ensure privacy from nosy (we mean thoughtful, conscientious) neighbors. For some extra flair, put up some tiki torches and a little thatched hut to create an exotic hideaway.

113. Make love in some secluded mountain meadow in bright sunshine or at twilight. Use the trunk of the car for a level spot for a romantic encounter down some dirt road in the middle of the desert.

114. Buy some clay and sculpt a model of your mate. Place the model in some private place where he or she (but not the rest of the world) will see it on a regular basis (inside a drawer or closet). If you are a little brave, do an abstract art piece of a part of his or her body. You might be able

to set this one out because only the two of you will know what it really is.

115. Rent an old-fashioned romantic movie and pick up the story line someplace in the middle. In the forties, sex was not allowed on the big screen (even if the characters were married). At the moment in the film when you think they might have succumbed to their passions, turn off the flick, and go finish the story line in your room.

116. Create a time capsule of your love. Place pieces of clothing, love notes, and pictures into a tin and mark it "Evidence of Our Red-Hot Monogamy." Date it with your names and year and bury it in the backyard. Mark your Palm Pilot or calendar for ten or twenty years so that you can dig it up, or simply leave it so that centuries from now, some unsuspecting anthropologist will find evidence that married couples had hot sex.

117. Write erotic poetry together. You write a line, then have your spouse add a line, then you add to it, and so on. See what kind of sonnet to your love you can create. Read the final version aloud to each other (perhaps reenacting some of the best parts of the poem).

118. Compete at something: checkers, pool, a swim race. The winner gets his or her pick of a sexual joy. There is nothing like a little healthy competition to get the sparks flying.

119. Create a love letter by cutting words out of magazines and pasting them onto a page. (Or a living love letter; paste them on to each other and then read the letter.)

120. See if you can locate a drive-in movie theater (a few really do still exist) and enjoy a heavy make-out session.

121. Take a sentimental journey. Recount or reenact your top ten favorite sexual moments of your married life.

122. Give your mate one of something for every year you have been married: one long stem rose per year, one pearl to complete a necklace, one collectible item for his or her collection, one kiss...be creative.

123. Do partner yoga stretching. Gently lift her leg, pull his arms forward or back. Sit facing each other with feet touching in a straddle and seesaw back and forth to stretch out your mate. Have her do a "downward dog" (toe touch), then you do one right over the top of her, body to body, over her back. You can (and should) leave out the Eastern mysticism. To add zip, do it naked.

124. Write love messages on your spouse's back with your fingernail or the gentle touch of your finger, and see if he or she can guess what you are saying.

125. Pray as you are enjoying each other sexually. You can pray things such as, "Lord, thank You for my husband's strength" as you stroke his bicep. Feel free to also pray and be grateful for inner character qualities and attributes as well.

6

Come on, Baby, Light My Fire, Part 2

CREATIVE CONNECTIONS

It is possible to fan the flame of a heart from which life has stolen a sense of hope. Romance can rise even from the ashes of grief. When a person truly loves, he or she looks for a powerful way to say "I will be there for you." Denise shares one poignant action that renewed her ability to love again:

> One day my husband, Mark, carved *I love you* in our kitchen cutting board. Years later Mark became ill with cancer and then passed away. Steve, a good single friend to Mark and me, kept contact with me and the kids to see how we were doing. Steve was a part of our small group Bible study too. Steve and I fell in love

and were married. Steve was good to keep Mark in conversations with the kids. He never felt that he had to compete with Mark. One year for Christmas, after a move to a new house, I opened up a gift. Inside was the cutting board with the *I love you* that Mark had carved. Steve had added photos of Mark with me and Mark with the kids, and he had it made into a beautiful wall hanging.

The flames of red-hot monogamy can be fanned. You can experience passion and excitement again, even after a broken heart, after grief, and after a season of being alone. Give love a chance by choosing to become a lover who gives. Passion will boomerang back so you reap the benefits of sizzling sex too!

This chapter is a continuation of the traits of a red-hot lover. When a lover is truly caring for you, he or she will keep your best interests in mind. Love is doing what is best for the other person regardless of the cost to self. One of the best gifts you can give to fan the flame is the gift of believing the best about your mate. It is easy to pick out all the negatives in yourself and your spouse. The real gift is in choosing to highlight the positive.

Attentive

This trait of a red-hot lover takes a little work. Check out Sol and Sunny. In Song of Songs chapter 2, we see that they are attentive to each other.

She says, "I am a rose of Sharon, a lily of the valleys" (Song of Songs 2:1). A lily was a common flower, like a dandelion. Sunny is feeling a bit unworthy to be queen, a little self-conscious.

He says, "Like a lily among thorns is my darling among the maidens" (verse 2). Meaning all the other women are like thorns compared to you, baby!

She responds, "Like an apple tree among the trees of the forest is my lover among the young men. I delight to sit in his shade, and his fruit is sweet to my taste" (verse 3).

How many apple trees do you find a forest? That's right. She is saying that her lover is one in a million. When you are attentive, you seek to meet the underlying need in each other's heart. Needs such as security, confidence, and encouragement. You'll want to put on your detective hat, pick up on a few clues, and take a few notes. Observe a few things.

Observe the joy. What makes him or her smile? What makes your spouse bubble with enthusiasm? What news does your spouse perceive as "good news"? What makes her say, "Aw, that's sweet"? Or him say, "Awesome! Incredible!" What circumstances would your mate describe as "fantastic"?

Observe the stress and the stress relievers. What makes your mate's neck knot up? What stressors tense up his shoulders? What makes her forehead wrinkle and leave her rubbing her temples? What issues make him have a shorter fuse or provoke a harsher tone? Is there some inner fear or frustration that is contributing to her temperament ? Is there some loss or grief that is contributing to a mood change?

In the same way, what makes him or her calm down and relax? What activities lower the intensity level and bring more peace to the home front? What causes your spouse to stroll rather than power walk? What turns their mood from task oriented to stopping to smell the roses?

Observe the responsibility. Are you in a season of life that carries a lot of pressure (parents of toddlers, teens; a midlife couple paying for colleges, cars, weddings; and caring for your own health issues and perhaps aging parents as well)?

Is there some deadline at work, at church, or in your community volunteer work that is raising adrenaline levels? Is some extra responsibility, such as getting a higher degree or coping with a tough teen, causing your mate to feel depressed, angry, or despondent?

Observe the pleasure. Does a certain small gesture or touch move your mate's readiness level for sex? Does a certain amount of time spent together do it? A certain conversation? A certain amount of listening by you, helping by you, or encouragement from you outside the bedroom that makes him or her more amorous and responsive?

During lovemaking, what causes your spouse to whisper, "I love when you do that" or purr with contentment? What makes him or her breathe heavier? What brings about a sigh? God designed us to make noise during foreplay and intercourse, so use it to your advantage.

Dr. Kevin Leman wrote a book titled *Sex Begins in the Kitchen.* His main premise is that what turns a woman on has very little to do with what happens in the bedroom. I regularly ask women at women's conferences what really turns them on (what is the true aphrodisiac?). A few of the most memorable responses are:

- When he does the dishes.
- When he arranges for the babysitter.
- When he gets down on the floor and plays Barbie with my girls.
- When he runs the errand or picks up the kids from soccer.
- When he says, "Thanks for dinner. It was great!"
- When he says, "Let me give the kids a bath. I know you wanted to work on…"
- When he takes out the trash. (How's that for foreplay?)

The amount of sex a man gets in the bedroom is directly related to how helpful and attentive he is in all the other rooms of the house.

Gentlemen, start your engines! What gets a man's attention and prepares him for great sex? Show up naked! Okay, he is a little deeper than that. To sum it up, men are driven to be successful. This does not mean that all men want to be rich or corporate leaders. It does, however, mean that men only like to engage in activities they believe they can succeed in. They will tackle any challenge, climb any height, and practice any skill as long they are confident they can succeed. As a result, here are statements men have made to me that made them more interested in their wives:

- She believes in me, even if others have doubts.
- She still flirts with me, even though we have been married for years.
- She accepts the fact that I don't have a way to turn off my sex drive.
- She has friends to talk with, so I don't have to be the only one who listens to her.
- She cooperates financially, so there are very few surprises with our money.
- She gets herself in the mood, so I know she is interested in me.

Self-Aware

You need a bit of biological information in your mind in order to be a truly red-hot lover. To experience orgasm, for one, you have to know what it is and what it feels likes. One sex therapist explains, "It is hydraulics and tension." Basically, the body builds up tension and then looks for a way to relieve the internal pressure. It is kind of like teakettles that whistle. When the water gets boiling hot, everybody in the house knows about it.

Another sex therapist likened orgasm and climax to "surrender." As he explained, his emotions carried him further, and he likened it to a releasing, a giving over, and then he chimed in, "Like the song, 'I Surrender All.'" Having heard that explanation, I sing that hymn with a big smile, knowing that God rejoices when couples commit and trust one another enough to really let go and surrender. We liken that moment of orgasm to the safe feeling that gives a small child the freedom to jump off a diving board into his or her loving parent's arms. Surrendering to the moment of orgasm means the atmosphere was conducive to complete trust. Orgasm can come when we say, "I trust my husband, I trust my body, I trust the privacy of this bed. I trust God to bless this act of marriage, and I trust myself enough to allow full enjoyment of the moment."

In the Mood?

You will be a much better lover if you become aware of the way your body responds sexually to life. Men, are you aware of what is going on in your mind and in your environment when your penis becomes erect? Are there patterns you can identify, or is it just one of life's mysteries? Are you conscious of what you say to your wife that causes a rise in your affection? Are you alert to the activities that cause your sexual interest to grow?

Ladies, are you attentive to the increase in vaginal mucus that takes place at certain times during the month? This is your body signaling you that you are ready to be more fertile. God has designed your sexual desire to increase at this time of the month. Your husband is more attractive, and sexual activity will be more appealing. Your emotional energy is more positive, your breasts are more responsive, and there is more lubrication available to make sex more enjoyable.

Later we'll discuss the mechanics, biology, and responsibilities of sex—the more clinical stuff. But for right now, close your eyes and think about your favorite times of sexual intimacy with your mate. What stands out? (We suggest that you and your spouse lie naked in the bed and do this exercise silently but at the same time, because it usually produces a desire for some red-hot monogamy.)

Ready? In your mind's eye, picture your body. What would you like your red-hot lover to do as he or she:

> Touches your head?
> Shoulders?
> Arms?
> Hands and fingers?
> Chest/breasts?
> Stomach, hips?
> Thighs?
> Legs?
> Feet and toes?

Now turn over. How about:

> Your back?
> Shoulders?
> The small of your back?
> Bottom?

Now open up a bit more.

Men, how do you like to be touched on your penis? Scrotum? The space between your genitals and anus?

Women, how do you like to be touched on your inner thigh? On the pelvic region? On the labia and then on into the vagina and clitoris?

As your eyes are closed, think about the movements, the touch, the talk, the use of your partner's hands or other body parts that have really sent you into orbit in the past. Or think about what he or she might have glanced by and you'd like more of. Or what was begun that you'd like carried further to the finish line?

What makes you breathe harder? Faster? What makes your heart race? What makes your mind leave today's responsibilities and enter that place of ecstasy? What makes you calm or purr (or howl or squeal) with delight? What produces the "Oh, yes! Oh, baby!" What makes the headboard rattle against the wall?

We should also see being a student of ourselves as a stewardship we give to our spouse. No human has the ability to read a mind, so there are only a few ways your spouse will know what pleases you:

- Verbally tell them.
- Show them.
- Give nonverbal, positive responses that are very clear.

In an area as vital to marital wellness as sexual intimacy, why make it a guessing game? Make a commitment to learn to express your desires. In fact, do this exercise together and begin today to express what you enjoy most.

Mature

A red-hot lover will do whatever it takes to grow in the area of intimacy. This might mean a young groom making his way into a women's lingerie department to buy that first Valentine's nightie. Or it might mean being open to being tutored by your mate and kissing him the way he likes it. It can mean taking mutual responsibility for contraception. It can mean attending OB/GYN appointments when your wife is pregnant. It can include reading, studying, or going to conferences to gain new skills, answer questions, or simply to renew the romance.

Vulnerability is the key to mature red-hot monogamy. Each partner must be able to openly, honestly, and clearly express his or her desires. A mature love knows the difference between wishes and desires, as well as the difference between boundaries and walls.

Desires are in your heart and mind and may or may not have been expressed verbally. A wish is the hope that a desire would be fulfilled. To move something from a desire or a wish, you need to express it to your mate. On the other hand, there may be something you want to change in your love life, and to initiate change, you need to be skillful at setting boundaries.

In setting boundaries, watch out for the two main counterfeits—wishes and walls. As stated, wishes are requests on your part for someone else to change. Walls are an attempt to protect a sensitive area of life. Let's take the example of our date night to illustrate the difference:

Boundary: We have set aside Thursday night as our date night.

Wish: You need to take me out on a date more often.

Wall: If we don't spend more time together, I'm not going to make it. (The spouse shuts down emotionally or creates distractions or diversions or in some cases punishments that further complicate an already hurtful area in the relationship.)

As you can see, the boundary is clear and easy to evaluate. It is simple to schedule, simple to agree on, and simple to implement. The wish, on the other hand, is not only vague but dependent on someone else. Your spouse must first figure out what you mean by this statement and then decide if it is worth the effort to address a need that is not very clear. The wall is the most ineffective, and most destructive, of the three. It is so vague it is impossible for your spouse to figure it out. The worst part, however, is the drastic tone of the statement.

Sometimes one partner has a habit or pattern that is destructive to the relationship and it leaks into the bedroom. Boundaries are a clear statement of the action one partner will take if his or her spouse is not taking steps to change. For example:

She says: If you yell and swear at me, I will walk out of the room because that is not how God wants you to talk to me. I don't want to allow you to do things that will cause a further rift in our relationship. I love you, so when you swear, I will walk away. (Then do it.)

He says: When you overspend, my desire for you wanes, so let's brainstorm a plan to keep your spending in line with what we can afford, and if you do not cooperate, then I will (state a clear consequence).

She says: I love us too much to let pornography come between us. Because I love us and I love what we've had in the past in our sex life, I want to team with you to protect it. Here's the phone. Please call someone you trust who can help us. (If he doesn't call, then you call a counselor for you.)

Boundaries move the relationship to health. Walls are the opposite; they further contribute to the problem by uses of manipulations and punishments that cause harm (such as derogatory statements, tone of voice, sarcasm). Because intimate relationships are highly emotional, one reaction can breed other reactions. The tone of a statement could give rise to unhealthy responses, which will encourage more unhealthy reactions. As a result, walls are always self-defeating and leave everyone frustrated. For example, if your mate is slow to respond to your sexual suggestions, a wall would be to say, "Well, I just won't give any sex until he or she does things my way." That's like shooting yourself in the foot. You are hurting yourself and the relationship in the very area you wanted to cause change. "Change" is the operative word. Sometimes the change is caused through choices we make, and sometimes change is initiated by our reactions to some common seasons every marriage goes through.

There are different stages of growth that every couple experiences in their lifelong journey of love. These stages are vital to the long-term health of your relationship because life does not remain static. Over time, your body changes, your responsibilities change, your sense of purpose changes, and your energy level changes. The bad news is that each of these changes makes life more challenging. The good news is that you can discover a new relationship with your spouse over and over again. Life will change with or without your cooperation. If you choose to mature along the way, you will discover new depths in your ability to become a red-hot lover.

Young Lovers

The first stage of an intimate relationship happens when you are young, in love, and full of hopes and dreams. You have not yet explored your sexual potential and everything is new. You experience your first highly passionate kiss, your first venture into foreplay, and your first time of intercourse. This is an exciting and unnerving time in life. It is exciting because you are discovering so many new things. You are intensely curious about the way your spouse was created. You wonder what it must be like to be the other person. As a man, you are fascinated with your wife's breasts and the beauty of her body. Her vagina is a wonderful mystery, and her sexual response is fascinating. Ejaculation is like nothing you have ever experienced before, and you can't seem to get enough. As a woman, you are enamored with your husband's strength and focus on you. You are curious about his penis but a little embarrassed. You are amazed at how differently your body responds compared to his. You are glad your husband desires you but wish he would be more patient.

This is also a time in life when you discover new potential in yourself. As a woman, you slowly become aware of your sexual possibilities. You will probably experience your first orgasm during this phase. Prior to that experience, you view sex as a satisfying time together and something nice you do for your husband. With your first orgasm, however, you discover there is a lot more to this sexual journey than just your husband's satisfaction. As a man, you quickly become aware of your ability to be incredibly active sexually. You discover a nearly insatiable appetite for your wife's body and enter an interesting challenge of self-control. You feel the pressure build up in your groin on a regular basis and relish the opportunity to release. When inter-course is not possible for a number of days, you discover a new level of frustration. You get angry over the littlest things and have very little patience with anything that keeps you from having sex. You realize you cannot live this way, so you begin looking for ways to bring your sexual desire under your control. You also begin hoping your wife becomes more interested in sex and that somehow she can understand this glorious struggle in your life. You work hard to keep sex in its proper perspective so it does not take over all your decisions.

This is the stage of exploration. You are introduced to an inti-mate relationship and challenge yourself to be vulnerable enough to be a proficient sexual partner. The goals of this stage are to build trust and develop healthy ways of being curious about each other. Trust is developed through good communication skills, especially listening, and respecting one another's decisions. You are merging your lives together, and you both approach life dif-ferently. As you share your convictions, preferences, desires, and fears, you gain insight into one another. As you respect one an-other's ways of approaching life, you give the message that he or she is safe with you. It is as if you are saying to one another, "You can share your dreams, your hopes, your fears, and your hidden desires with me and I will treasure them. You can make mistakes around me and I will forgive you. You can explore life with me. I will rejoice over the victories, and I will laugh with you over our embarrassments. You can be who you are around me."

For most newlyweds, one of the biggest concerns is enjoying sex without having the worry of pregnancy. Many couples prefer to plan the timing of parenthood. In today's market there are nu-merous options: barrier methods, such as condoms, diaphragms, or IUDs; hormonal methods, such as an oral contraceptive, a patch, or implants; natural family planning (this method gives the advantage of learning your own body well, so when you do want to become pregnant and are looking for your most fertile time, you already know it). Then there are permanent options, such as vasectomy and tubal ligation. No method is perfect. They all have their pluses and minuses.

You will want to talk through the physical and biological impact each have on your bodies (most impact the woman's body), and what impact each would have on your relationship. Most importantly, you'll want to discuss the moral comfort levels you have with various methods of birth control. (To have the moral discussion, investigate how each method actually works. We felt uncomfortable using anything that would end a pregnancy after the egg is fertilized because the moment of conception creates a new life. As you gain more information, your choices may change. We have used five different methods over our 25 years together.) Newlyweds might feel more comfortable with options that allow more spontaneity. Stopping to put on a condom or waiting for sex until you are less fertile might feel like a bigger negative earlier in your relationship.

After a sexual adjustment is made, you might be more comfortable with your own body and the sexual act, making other options something to consider at this point. You can share responsibility for contraception. For example, if you decide on condoms, she can undo the package and roll it lovingly on to his penis. If you both decide on the Pill or a patch, he can bring you the water and the pill daily or place the patch on as a part of your lovemaking.

This is also a time when you discover the real influence your family has had on you. If your family was secure, you are probably going to be secure in this new relationship. If your family was chaotic and unpredictable, you will probably feel a need to create chaotic interactions between you and your spouse. If your family was harsh, you will discover a growing harshness in this new relationship. If your family was abusive, you will discover a block in your ability to attain true intimacy. This often confuses people because these traits lie dormant in our lives until we say "I do." These are the characteristics of intimacy that were emotionally programmed into your life by the people who loved you the most in your childhood. These traits do not necessarily show up in friendships, ministry, or work relationships.

With the commitment to enter a sexual relationship, the door is opened wide for these deep-seated qualities to surface. If these characteristics are healthy, you get a head start in your marriage. You will still need to grow to adjust to them because they are "new" based on a new stage in life, but the adjustment will be gradual and relatively simple. If these traits, however, are unhealthy, your need to grow is intense. These qualities are challenging to the relationship and can be destructive to your future.

The Test

This was an intense time in our life because Pam was raised in an unpredictable, alcoholic home. For her, love was mixed with great admiration and chaotic reactions. I was raised in a home with a controlling mom who was afraid of most things. As a result, I became more passive than I should be and Pam was more dramatic than she should be. We first noticed these traits on our honeymoon. It was our last night and neither of us wanted it to end. Pam started telling me about every boyfriend she had ever had, starting with fifth grade.

Rather than work out a deal to have this conversation on our three-hour drive to the airport the next day, I passively said, "Okay." But in the middle of her dating biography I feel asleep. I woke to Pam sobbing while she was saying, "You don't love me anymore. You have already lost interest in me!" I was embarrassed at myself, so I reassured her I was still intensely interested. She stopped crying, thanked me, and asked if she could sing her favorite country western songs to me. Our honeymoon ended with Pam standing on our bed singing "Stand by Your Man," followed by two and a half hours of sleep before we drove out of the mountains in a snowstorm. I truly believe we would have worn each other out if we had not committed to a deliberate plan for growth that has counteracted the chaotic influence of our pasts.

We tell couples all the time that everything changes when you get married, but most people don't believe us. Tom and Jan are a good example. They were part of the crowd that believed living together before marriage is a good idea. They believed they could test out their relationship first and go to the altar with confidence. Well, prior to the wedding, their relationship worked pretty well. They laughed a lot together and respected one another's careers and commitments. They had no complaints about their intimate life. Then they got married. Within two weeks, their insecurities erupted.

Jan had been abandoned by every significant male in her life, including her father and grandfather. After Tom arrived home one day, Jan accused him of being a liar and ran everything through that filter. Everything he said from that point on became evidence that proved her point. Tom had a string of broken relationships in his past and very little respect for his mom. Rather than responding with compassion, Tom accused Jan of being crazy and completely out of control. They were surrounded with supportive friends and had access to counseling, but they chose to do what felt right to them. They refused to commit to aggressive growth, and their relationship ended a few weeks after their ceremony with pain and confusion on both sides. They appear to be doing well as individuals today because the issues have once again gone dormant.

The Parenting Years

At some point, each couple makes the decision whether to become parents. We know that some couples will choose not to become parents, which brings its own issues, but we are going to focus on those who have chosen to add to their family simply because it is a bigger group. If you choose not to have children, we recommend you look for a mentor couple who has taken this same road and ask God to give you special insight into His plan for your life, as you will have opportunities and options not available to most couples.

I (Bill) will never forget the night we became parents. Pam had a different look in her eyes. She knew she was fertile, she knew we were secure, and she knew we were ready, even though I wasn't exactly sure. She approached our lovemaking with a fervor and confidence I had not seen before. I can still picture the room we were in, the window, the lighting, and the look of anticipation in her eyes. As we lay back quietly in bed, the realization hit me. *We are going to be parents. What we just did is going to result in a baby!* I was scared, excited, overwhelmed, and proud all at the same time. I know it is not that straightforward for everyone, but the reactions are usually similar. We are exhilarated and exhausted at the thought of taking on responsibility for another life. We begin to discover a new level of ability in our lives. We are more patient than we thought possible. We have a deeper capacity to care about other human beings than we had ever dreamed. We can work harder, feel deeper, focus more intensely, and dream bigger.

It is as if pregnancy is a shadow of things to come. The first three months are generally exhausting for the new mom. Morning sickness and hormonal changes lower her energy level. This is just like raising toddlers. Young children are needy and busy. As a result, parents of toddlers get less sleep than they need and give of themselves constantly.

The second three months are a time of intense energy. Something kicks into gear, and the young mother becomes a relentless whirlwind of energy. She can clean tirelessly, redecorate anything in her path, and have sex over and over again. I (Bill) am still amazed at my inability to keep up with Pam during the second trimester each time she was pregnant. It was humbling but necessary to say to her, "I just can't do it again. I am sorry." This is a good foreshadowing of the years after your kids enter elementary school but before their teen years. As parents, you regain some control over your schedule because you are not chasing kids all day long. They have their own schedules, but they are relatively manageable. At the same time, a wife's sexual drive reaches its peak around 30 years old. Her appetite for sex increases, so she becomes more adventurous in the bedroom, and the couple has some time to enjoy this new discovery.

The primary goal during the elementary years is to set up healthy boundaries. Life is filling with options that are all vying for your attention. If you do not have boundaries, your love life will get squeezed out. You will have traded red-hot monogamy for lukewarm monotony. Boundaries are decisions you make to maintain self-respect in your life. Self-respect can be summed up as doing what is truly in your best interest. It is not a commitment to be selfish; rather, it is a commitment to live a healthy, balanced life. Pam and I were able to maintain these boundaries primarily because we had a date night every week.

We trained our kids to go to bed early on these nights and traded babysitting with friends to ensure they could have a weekly date night also. We found we had a greater capacity for all of life when we stayed connected in our romantic, sexual life.

The third trimester is just exhausting. Mom is overloaded with extra weight, questions about her ability to be a successful mom, and a growing sense that people are depending on her. She is physically tired and emotionally on edge. Her life is getting bigger by the day, and she hopes she is up for the challenge. This is a good picture of the teen years. Teens begin to make their own plans, and they make commitments to who they want to be in life. They often have complex schedules and lofty financial needs. As parents, you will need to work hard to keep up with their needs and be available on their timetable. At the same time, your parents may be getting older and need added attention from you as well. All these people in your life at this time are unpredictable and can throw your life into a tailspin. This time of life requires more of you than any other.

The primary goal when teens are still at home is to clarify your priorities. Priorities give you a strong sense of what is really important. We often end up having one priority which includes everything. Since it is impossible to keep up with everything, we live with the agonizing conclusion that we have worked incredibly hard and still feel like failures. To help you clarify your priorities, draw a large triangle on a blank piece of paper. On the bottom line of the triangle, write down the ten most important parts of your life. Then draw a line over the words and rewrite the list again, but this time leave one of them off. Understand, you are not eliminating anything because all ten of these are important. You are simply trying to get a better handle on how these priorities impact your life. Repeat this process until you just have one priority at the top of the triangle. Next time you have to make a decision or a commitment, look over this priority triangle and ask yourself, "Is this decision consistent with my priorities?"

The Victory Stage

By their very nature, intimate relationships expose us. Not only do we spend time with one another while we are physically naked, we expose ourselves spiritually and emotionally as well. As a result, sexual intimacy will bring our struggles to the surface. If you have taken the courageous step of giving yourself to your spouse and there are problems from your past, you will be confronted with them. At this point, you will either face them and discover a remarkable victory, or you will resist change and ruin the relationship that helped you identify your need to grow. It is our prayer that you choose to grow. It is beyond the scope of this book to deal with these obstacles in detail, but we present here the introductory steps to help you get on the path of victory.

The first possibility is that you will face physical difficulties. Early in a marriage, premature ejaculation for men and painful intercourse for women are common. As a couple, you long to be together but you can grow frustrated when he releases before she can catch up. Or you find yourselves inhibited because you don't know what to do about the pain. If this is your story, take some time to read *Intended for Pleasure* together. It is written by a doctor and gives sound advice with practical exercises to help you navigate these common maladies. If the exercises in the book do not help, be sure to consult a physician to ensure that nothing abnormal is going on. Please do not be embarrassed. These are common obstacles that can be solved in most cases.

As you grow older, other physical problems can develop. Early in the marriage, it is impossible for a man to ever think he will see the day he will be unable to achieve an erection. The flood of commercials for erectile dysfunction medication is evidence of just how common this is. Added stress, fatigue, growing demands, and physical changes in a man's body can all create situations where an erection just does not happen. It is always best to see your doctor if this happens more than a few times. For women, from periods to PMS to menopause, your life is in constant flux. These changes are hormonal, physical, and frustrating. They can create a number of situations in which sexual activity is uncomfortable. Honestly communicating with your OB/GYN is the best course of action.

SEXY, RED, AND RACY

Every step of maturity brings new possibilities. I (Pam) am a speaker for Hearts at Home, an organization that encourages mothers. One year at the conference, the emcee, Julie Ann Barn-hill, brought down the house with her suggestion that life just looks better when you are wearing "sexy, little, red, racy under-wear." You should have seen the sea of thousands of nodding heads when she held up those tiny, lacy panties! All the women laughed and smiled in agreement, giving that knowing response. Sometimes you just have to take responsibility to get yourself into the right mood and frame of mind! So whether it's buying some racy red panties, setting aside time to actually do the activi-ties in this book, scheduling a counseling appointment, or simply carving out time to rest in each other's arms in a hammock and watch a sunset, do something today to step up (or lay down) and make red-hot monogamy a priority.

Here are some ways to get the kids to cooperate so you can get in some time for romance:

1. Toss all your change into the greenery in the backyard and tell them they can keep any coins they can find.

2. Do an Easter egg hunt all year round. Hide a desig-nated number of eggs (plastic work well with toys, candy, or coins inside). Tell your children that no one can come inside the house until all the eggs are found (take one egg out so they can't find the last one). When you are finished, bring the last egg out and ask, "Were you looking for this one?"

3. For toddlers: Get a favorite video going (be sure to check the time—you might have 30 minutes or two hours!). For older kids: Rent or buy a new video. Use a realistic line like, "Mom and Dad are taking some grown-up time" "Mom and Dad are going to take a nap." Or our favorite: "We are going to clean our room and can't be interrupted." (After sex, you'd better hurry and pick up your room!) For teens: Give them movie tickets so the house is yours for a night.

4. Trade time off with your friends so that each of you has a few hours a week alone. Or, since we are pastors, we can get away with recommending this: Send the kids to a youth group or Sunday school activity, have sex, and then meet them at church later. (We'll just call this worshipping at Bedside Baptist.) If this tip is used occasionally, your pastor won't mind because you will have a strong marriage and family and that makes for a strong church.

5. Hire a neighborhood sitter an ask her to take the kids to her home to watch the kids for a few hours.

6. When the movie is playing in the living room, tell the kids you are going to clean the garage. Lock the garage door on your way out and enjoy some sex in the backseat of your car. Or hide in a closet and kiss until one of the kids finally finds you.

7. Recruit Grandma to take the kids for ice cream or to McDonald's—or for an extra treat, ask her to take them to the zoo all day.

8. Enroll the kids in preschool and arrange for you and your spouse to go in late to work once a week.

9. Take a long lunch once a week on a school day. Block off from noon till two or three. Write in the calendar: Appointment, R.H.M. (Your secretary won't know it stands for red-hot monogamy.)

10. Take advantage of those precious hours kids sleep. The dishes can wait. When Junior nods off, head to the bedroom first, and then go back to responsibilities. Or wake each other up in the early morning for sex, or in the middle of the night just start fondling your spouse, and he or she will most likely wake up. You'll get less sleep, but at least you'll be smiling the next day anyway.

Hands-on Homework

$\mathcal{E}$ach of you take ten minutes to write a love letter in response to this statement: When I think of the traits of a red-hot lover—someone who is others centered, a risk taker, God focused, attentive, self-aware, and mature—the trait on the list that I think captures your strength so well is _____ . And that makes me feel _____ .

Now sit facing each other on the bed completely naked, and take turns reading your love letters to each other. After you both finish, take a few minutes to sit entwined, face-to-face, and gaze into each other's eyes.

Red-Hot
ROMANCE IDEAS

126. Praise each other from head to toe. Stand completely naked facing each other and take turns caressing and kissing body parts from the bottom up or vice versa. Be sure to say what you enjoy or find arousing or interesting about the various areas of each other's bodies.

127. Dream and pray together. Take a walk on the beach or some scenic setting and talk or pray through hopes and dreams. Great sex begins by revealing who we really are deep down.

128. If she is experiencing PMS, run her a bath and float rose petals in it. Get her some chocolate and her favorite Christian romance novel. She just might get back in the mood, but it would be best to give with no immediate expectations.

129. Look at your wedding album and talk about what first attracted you to your mate.

130. Dave Arp, coauthor of *No Time for Sex,* shared a clever idea. When his wife, Claudia, was at an appointment, he left a note on the windshield of her car, "Would the owner of this car hurry to 8624 Dovetail Drive to meet your lover for a romantic rendezvous?"

131. See how long you can kiss continuously.

132. Kiss every time you see something specific (at red lights, when you spot a fire hydrant, anytime you see your favorite flower or hear your favorite song). Dave and Claudia

Arp, marriage specialists, kiss whenever they see a body of water. We kiss on every elevator we find ourselves alone in, and we kiss and dance after we push the elevator button and are waiting for it to arrive.

133. Buy matching bathrobes. Go on a pajama shopping date (be sure to model the options—or at least provide a quick private peek).

134. Flirt a little. Run your bare foot up his pant leg, run your finger down his arm, reach over and place your hand high up on the thigh...make a move.

135. Carefully tease. A few inside jokes, some light banter, sharing a few laughs all ring the sexual tension up a notch that will need to find its release in some red-hot monogamy.

136. Read jokes to each other. Couples that play together, stay together.

137. Find a new sport or hobby to learn together. When you both look awkward and stupid, it bonds you.

138. Add romance to the routine. Leave a love note in his coffee cup so he sees it first thing every morning. Add a flower when you bring in the morning paper. Talk about pleasant sexual memories as you make the bed together in the morning. Get a greeting card when you run to the grocery store.

139. "How do I love thee? Let me count the ways." Write on a set of index cards all the reasons you love your spouse. Make a paper chain of her or his best qualities. Buy a flower for each positive trait you want to recount, and give them to her one at a time as you verbally list off what makes your heart sing.

140. Match up. You might think this is a little hokey, but buy something that matches: coffee cups, T-shirts, bikes, pajamas, rings, etc.

141. Skip the pajamas all together—matching or not! Go to bed dressed in your best self.

142. Write on the bathroom mirror in the middle of the night a message like "You look beautiful!" or "What a gorgeous hunk!"

143. If you have a really trusted girlfriend, take turns snapping pictures of each other in your husband's favorite "outfit" or lingerie. Make the lens a soft focus, and create a photo album for your husband. (If you each use your own digital camera, then you retain control over the pictures.) There are also reputable professional photographers who do these kinds of photos. Just make sure the studio is in a safe neighborhood and the photographer is trustworthy and of a good reputation. (I'd still take a friend to be on the safe side—plus, if she did it too for her husband, we both might be more courageous!)

144. If you are a woman who travels, take along a dress shirt your husband has worn that still has his scent and cologne smell on it, and sleep in the shirt. Absence really will make your heart grow fonder.

145. Play "Kato." (Kato is the houseboy from the *Pink Panther* movies who attacks Inspector Clouseau when he doesn't expect it.) When you are both in bed and have said goodnight, one partner—without the other knowing—slips out of bed and crawls around the foot of the bed and grabs the other partner or attacks him or her with a hug (or other expressions of affection). Be careful with this one. You don't want your spouse to mistake you for a robber

or intruder! Keep it light. One woman who tried this gave herself away. Her husband knew something was going to happen as she giggled all the way around the bed before reaching out for him in the dark.

146. Wear something sexy under your clothes to work to help you remember all day that you want to be with your spouse all night.

147. Wear your pajamas all day together (if you are empty nesters or newlyweds with no children, wear nothing all day together). If you go with the second option, be sure to close the blinds.

148. Go on an old-fashioned hayride.

149. Go on a carriage ride or sleigh ride.

150. Give romantic gifts at unexpected times. In *Romancing Your Husband,* Debra White Smith suggests 12 unique ways to romance your mate for the 12 days of Christmas. (The five gold rings might set you back a piece, but you can adapt the idea. Debra used gold garland with five love notes of her husband's best traits to make that day more affordable.) Don't just give the kids Easter baskets and Halloween pillow cases; instead place a little "grown up" something in a dime-store kid's basket and give it to your mate in the bedroom.

7

Sizzling Sex

IGNITING PASSION

ears ago Bill wrote a book called *Let Her Know You Love Her: 100 Ways to Make Your Wife's Day*. After the book was released, Bill was a guest on a radio program. This interview, however, was on a sports station. After the interview, I picked up the messages off our office phone. One was from a man who sounded a little desperate. "Hey, I just heard some guy on *Mighty Sports 90,* and he was talking about some book I need. I think it was something like *100 Ways to Make Your Old Lady's Day*. I think I need that book."

Yes, you definitely do! I sent it overnight express with a prayer that the first thing he'd apply is, "Don't call your wife 'old lady'!"

Well, if you are a lover who might have put your foot in your mouth once or twice, how can you learn to communicate feelings as personal as a desire for your mate?

LOVE TO LOVE YA, BABY

Come up with a way to clearly let your mate know you are interested. There are pillows that either say "Tonight" or, on the flip side, "Not Tonight." (I [Pam] have a pair of socks that say the same thing on the cuffs. My married son saw them in Bill's Christmas stocking and jokingly said, "If you need socks to get the message across, something is seriously wrong in the relationship, Mom.")

A few more ways to ask your mate if he or she is interested in sex might be:

- Do you want to make love?
- Are you interested?
- What are you doing for the next hour?
- So, do you want to do it?
- I'm interested. Do you have the energy?
- Would you like to be together?
- Are you asleep?
- Want to take a nap?

Our favorite unique expression for wanting sexual intimacy comes from a conference in the Deep South. Before we spoke, the conferees played their own unique version of *The Dating Game*. One of the questions was "What would be the perfect date?" All the guys replied, "Do (various dating activities: movie, dinner, etc.) and then come home early." One newlywed said, "Come home early and light a fire in the fireplace and a fire on the couch!" Then Bill and I got it—couples don't have "sex" in the South; they "come home early" and "light a fire on the couch"!

ENCRYPTED LOVE

Sometimes it is fun to create code words that let your spouse know you are interested. One counselor said her clients would ask, "Do you want to bake some cookies?" She wasn't sure what happened if the inquirer really did want to bake cookies. Perhaps sex was the only thing this couple baked up together.

We encourage people to have a code word to indicate a desire for sexual interaction. This is especially helpful after having children because life becomes more hectic. One couple shared how their code word evolved. It seems they were the parents of toddlers and life was a bit stressful. The husband's sister, who was single, volunteered to watch the kids so her brother and her sister-in-law could go on a date. Things were pretty tense, so most of the date was spent just walking and talking at the local lake. The couple picnicked and then continued to talk through life issues as they fed the ducks.

When they returned to the sister-in-law's to retrieve the children, she asked, "So how'd it go?"

Her brother said, "It was fine. Good. Thanks."

"Good, huh?" she asked, smiling. Her brother realized that his sister thought "good" meant they had taken the date time for sex, and he replied, "We just talked and fed the ducks."

"Fed the ducks, huh?"

The dad gathered the children and headed out to the car to meet his wife. After the kids were tucked into bed, he explained how his sister thought "Fed the ducks" was some code word for sex. To which she replied, "So, want to go feed the ducks?" For years now, this couple has been happily "feeding the ducks."

One couple we know buys a candle from every place they travel. When one of them is in the mood, it is very easy to read because all those candles are lit up as they walk in. "I'll light the candles" is their code.

Our most recent code word was born out of our book *Men Are Like Waffles—Women Are Like Spaghetti*. To understand the code word, you have to have a brief glimpse into the meaning of the book's title.

Men are like waffles. Men process life in boxes. If you look down at a waffle, you see a collection of boxes separated by walls. The boxes are all separate from each other and make convenient holding places. That is typically how a man processes life. A man's thinking is divided up into boxes that have room for one issue and one issue only. The first issue of life goes in the first box, the second goes in the second box, and so on. When a man is at work, he is at work. When he is in the garage tinkering around, he is in the garage tinkering around. When he is watching TV, he is simply watching TV. Social scientists call this "compartmentalizing."

Women are like spaghetti. In contrast to men's waffle-like approach, women process life more like a plate of spaghetti. If you look at a plate of spaghetti, you notice that individual noodles all touch one another. If you attempted to follow one noodle around the plate, you would intersect a lot of other noodles and you might even switch to another noodle seamlessly. That is how women face life. Every thought and issue is connected to every other thought and issue in some way. Life is much more of a process for women than it is for men. This is why a woman is typically better at multitasking than a man. She can talk on the phone, prepare a meal, make a shopping list, work on planning tomorrow's business meeting, give instructions to her children as they are going out to play, and close the door with her foot without skipping a beat.

When women are under stress, they like to talk their way through their feelings, often jumping from subject to subject. Men, on the other hand, like to go to their favorite easy boxes to recharge. God kind of clued women in a bit though, as most of men's favorite easy boxes are actually shaped like boxes: the TV, the computer screen, the newspaper, the football field, the basketball court, the baseball diamond, the tennis court, the garage, the refrigerator, and the bed. That bed box, the sex box, is kind of like the free square in the center of a bingo card, and a husband can get to that sex box from every other square in his waffle.

Well, after we had shared this at one conference, at any reference to sex the rest of the weekend, the conferees would say "Bingo!" During Saturday afternoon's free time, one couple went shopping and brought us back a gift they asked us to open in front of the crowd. The sign read "Born to Bingo!" So now at our home when one of us is feeling amorous, we ask, "Want to play some bingo?"

This code thing isn't just our clever idea. No, it was God's concept long ago. Check out our familiar sample couple, Sol and Sunny.

Solomon and his bride used code words for sexuality to build anticipation. For example, all references to "the garden" are references to the female sex organs. She says, "My lover has gone down to his garden, to the beds of spices, to browse in the gardens and to gather lilies" (Song of Songs 6:2). Then she adds, "I am my lover's and my lover is mine; he browses among the lilies" (6:3).

It is as if she is saying, "Honey, you are mine, and I am yours. I totally trust you, so browse. By all means, take your time, have your way with me. I am relaxed and confident in your love for me."

Some people are so shy that just the thought of asking their spouse for sex out loud is too stressful. One woman came up with a very unique solution to this dilemma. Every day before her husband came home from the office, she would write a number from one to ten on her side of the mirror, indicating her level of interest for that day. One meant "Not a chance" and ten meant "Where are you? I need you right now!"

MAKING YOUR DESIRES OBVIOUS

Sometimes you don't need words to get the message across. Debra White Smith, in her book *Romancing Your Husband,* shares a story of a day she arranged a lingerie scavenger hunt for her husband. Around town she had placed manila envelopes, and in each was a piece of lingerie! Also in each envelope was part of a love song as a clue, and directions as to whom to see and where to go to find the next envelope.

Another idea she gives is to tie a sequined bra to his steering wheel while it's parked in the driveway or at work. A note is not necessary.

Another way to prompt a sexual response is to meet a deep inner need in your mate. Debra's husband, Daniel Smith, shows in *Romancing Your Wife* that he understands a woman's need to be encouraged at her core. One morning the children of the Smith household asked, "Mommy, when are you going to put on your makeup?" Debra continued her usual routine and finally made her way into the bathroom. On the mirror, written with a dry erase pen, was "Picture Perfect" with a square right at the height to frame her face.

When a man speaks to a woman this way, he won't have to request sex very often because she'll automatically respond with some tangible love toward him.

WHAT'S OKAY TO ASK?

The number one question we are asked at marriage conferences is, "What's okay with God in the bedroom?" Couples want to fully experience all that God intended and also have a desire to avoid things that might undermine their relationship. When two lives come together, there are two different comfort levels with various aspects of sex. As people change over years of marriage, they grow in their interest in experimenting with new ideas in the area of red-hot monogamy. And in addition to all this, some come to the topic of sex with our own set of baggage: past hurts, misuse of sex, sexual abuse, or an ultra conservative upbringing that implied sex was "bad" or "dirty."

God seems to have given lots of freedom and just a few guidelines. Read on to see what we believe.

Sex Should Be Done out of Love, Never Forced

Very little is said in the Bible in the way of rules. There are principles, some which we have covered, such as: all lovemaking should be in a committed relationship of marriage (1 Thessalonians 4:3; Hebrews 13:4), each person should honor and respect the other (Ephesians 5), and our character should reflect Christ's with our focus on others and a heart of love that wants the best for our mate (Philippians 2).

The Song of Songs gives an attitude of freedom and delight and exploration as the ambiance God honors in marriage.

Sex Should Be Agreed Upon

Unity is a guiding principle in marriage that should also be a priority in the sexual area of your marriage.

- How good and pleasant it is when brothers live together in unity! (Psalm 133:1).

- May they be brought to complete unity to let the world know that you sent me and have loved them even as you have loved me (John 17:23).

- May the God who gives endurance and encouragement give you a spirit of unity among yourselves as you follow Christ Jesus (Romans 15:5).

- Make every effort to keep the unity of the Spirit through the bond of peace (Ephesians 4:3).

- As God's chosen people, holy and dearly loved, clothe yourselves with compassion, kindness, humility, gentleness and patience. Bear with each other and forgive whatever grievances you may have against one another. Forgive as the Lord forgave you. And over all these virtues put on love, which binds them all together in perfect unity (Colossians 3:12-14).

No sexual act, no matter how much it is desired by either of you, should be forced on the other. Selfish men sometimes pull out the submission verses and use them as a club over their wives to try to force their opinions on them. To do this is to wrench and twist the context of the submission section which also says husbands are to love their wives "as Christ loved the church" (Ephesians 5:25). Christ laid down His life for humankind. He considered us more important than His own life. A couple who wants to enjoy a lifetime of sexual satisfaction will seek to grow in their intimate expression to one another but will only engage in activities that are mutually agreed upon. Anything less than this will rob you of the very pleasure you are seeking.

On the flip side, be sure your resistance is not based on past baggage, a poor self-image, or an untrue view of what God blesses in marriage. If you are in doubt, pray it out. God will show you how to respond to your mate. God loves both of you and wants you to be fulfilled in this vital area of life.

Sex Should Be Just the Two of You

Here is an important guideline. God forbids mate swapping, multiple partners, and orgies. "Marriage should be honored by all, and the marriage bed kept pure, for God will judge the adulterer and all the sexually immoral" (Hebrews 13:4). Sex is a bond meant for only the two of you. Because it is just for two, this means all others, even pictures of others (pornography of any kind), are off limits.

What about sexual accouterments? Let's place these "extra ac-cessories" in two categories: (1) Neutral—These would be objects that do not in any way seek to replace a body part of your spouse. So things such as a bearskin rug, a silk scarf or fluffy boa, velvet or satin sheets, candles or oils, and most things you might wear would fall into this category. The things themselves are neu-tral—how they are used would then be the guiding principle. (2) Reproduction—If an accessory replaces your mate or the need for coitus, then that would undermine your unity or possibly alienate your mate, making it unhealthy. If it is something that draws you together, then it could be a possibility. The caution would be if you become accustomed to a substitute stimulation (as with a vibrator or dildo-type accouterment), then your body will not respond as well to your mate. Why settle for a represen-tation when you have the real thing and then learn to enhance that relationship? Why risk God's natural for some substitute?

If red-hot monogamy is for two, what about masturbation? This is an area that seems split among sex experts. Some say mas-turbation is always wrong because it is self-pleasure and leaves out your mate. Others allow for it when their partner is ill or in some other way (travel, disability, at-risk pregnancy) unable to meet the sexual need of a partner (with the partner's blessing on masturbation and it not being done behind his or her back). Still others say that masturbation can lead to information that can enhance a couple's sex life because as a person knows his or her body better, that information can then be shared with his or her spouse. Still others are fine with mutual stimulation to orgasm without intercourse (but then this isn't really masturbation any-more; it's extended foreplay).

There are definitely some vital cautions when discussing mas-turbation. Masturbation can become addictive. Some can become addicted to self-pleasure and then not long for their mate. They, in essence, short-circuit red-hot monogamy because the individual "cuts in line" in front of the marriage partner. Then, when the partner desires intercourse, the spouse is now uninterested because the immediate urge was fulfilled.

Masturbation can be fueled by fantasy, and often that fantasy doesn't focus on his or her mate but someone else, thus breaking the bonds of unity. And, in a few cases, a person can become so addicted to self-pleasuring that he or she avoids the sex act altogether with their mate or can't climax by his or her partner's actions.

Sex Should Be Something That Doesn't Risk Your Health or Life

People seem to come up with more and more ways to get a thrill out of the sex act, rather than relishing in the thrill of the relationship sex in marriage can give to two people. Some sexual practices will place one or both of you at risk. Any stimulants that impair your decision-making abilities will be counterproductive to your relationship. Other choices may be medically unwise (anal sex, and much of what is found in pornography, for example). If your spouse asks you to do anything that makes you feel derogated or frightened, or puts at risk your life and values, then you are free to say no! If there is any possibility that you might become sick or die as a result of an act of sex, then that sex act isn't worth it. FYI: Orgasm lasts 13 seconds for most men and 51 seconds for most women, so ask yourself, "Am I asking for or allowing a practice that would place the rest of what we love about our relationship and our life in any jeopardy or in harm's way for a few seconds of pleasure?"

POSITIONED FOR LOVE

While it is true that God gives only a few guidelines, there are some limitations based on biology and plumbing. There are only a few basic positions in which to enjoy red-hot monogamy, but each of these has all kinds of variations!

- *Man on top, woman on bottom, facing each other.* This is the familiar "missionary" position (called this because some natives on the Hawaiian Islands saw a missionary couple doing red-hot monogamy this way and they thought it odd). The missionary position can happen lying, sitting, or standing, but no matter how you slice it, the mechanics still work the same way. It is an easy position to adapt, especially for pregnancy, when she can slide to the edge of the bed and he can enter from a standing position, thus not lying on her tummy. (There are many ways to vary this face-to-face option.)

- *Man on bottom, woman on top.* (Man smiling because he likes the view. Woman smiling because orgasm is easier for her to achieve from this position.)

- *Side by side.* With the man in back so he can slide in, this position is often called spooning (another favorite in pregnancy as it can be more comfortable for mom-to-be).

- *Woman on bottom.* She is face down, either lying fairly flat, hips rotated a bit, or "cat/cow" position on all fours, with man on top and entering from the back. (The angle of this position can make ejaculation easier for a male.)

- *Man sitting, woman straddles him.* This is really a variance of the missionary position. Most any flat ledge will work for this: bed, desk, vanity counter, chair, etc.

- *Man standing, woman straddling him and being held by the man.* This one usually turns into another position very quickly because, even if the guy is a bench press champ, he is going to get distracted and will not want to "hold up" his end of the bargain forever. If he leans against a doorjamb or wall, he might last a little longer, but it's hard to relax and work out in this strenuous position at the same time, so it will be more of a quickie experience.

Pretty much everything else is just variations of these unless you are an Olympic gymnast or work for the circus. Variations can include things such as: wrapping your legs around his or her back (or for the very flexile, over the shoulders); changing the angle or pitch of the lovemaking; trying head to toe or toe to head; or straddle and face his feet instead of his face; but no matter what, the plumbing still meets in the middle. Sometimes you can vary the place more than the position (in a doorway, on a rocking chair, on the stairway, thus changing the angle up a bit). Or change the intensity or length of the experience. One sexual encounter might be hours long and relaxed, while the next might be minutes long and intense. Both can bring the desired result of sexual fulfillment and emotional connection.

We picked up a book that promised a new position for every day of the year (yep, drawings and everything), and it created more intimacy in our relationship, all right. Not because we tried all the positions (some Houdini couldn't even have mastered), but when we looked at some of the options, we just laughed and laughed together. Some looked as though they required a pulley system.

We believe that most couples, if they are willing to discuss their sexual preferences, will naturally discover all the positions they enjoy. Part of the fun of the positions is the fact that the two of you decided together to give it a try. The decision to get to know your mate and his or her body is the lasting adventure. And the commitment to both please your mate and allow yourself to release your desire is your great reward. When you are feeling amorous, express it (if you have the time and privacy), and you will discover all kinds of new ways of making love because you will be caught in unique places and positions: against a wall, kneeling, leaning up against some piece of furniture, etc. You don't need to have a manual—just a positive attitude, a desire to explore, and a little free time.

We appreciate Cliff and Joyce Penner's view in *The Gift of Sex:*

> A fun experience we recommend is for couples to find a book that has diagrams of various positions. Then plan a time...and have fun practicing getting your bodies into different positions without attempting entry. You could be nude, fully clothed, in underwear, or wearing whatever you wear to sleep. After this experiment, you might categorize the positions into (1) those you'd love to use for intercourse, (2) those you'd like to try but are not sure will actually be positive for you two, and (3) those that will never work for you.
>
> Develop an attitude of openness and freedom *so that you can let the choice of position grow out of the feelings of the moment... We like to think of letting positions evolve out of the experience, rather than getting into position, as if you were on the scrimmage line in a football game waiting for the whistle to blow"* (emphasis added).[1]

So much effort has gone into finding the right position, the right spot, the right technique. Men are looking for that place you can touch on a woman to drive her crazy—and there is one: *her heart.* A wife wants to please her husband and is wondering what is most effective. An attitude that is open to his needs is the best gift she can give. So while it is important to know the basics of biology and the sexual differences in the genders, it is more important to seek to really know the heart of your spouse. When you seek to be an encouragement, a blessing, and a helper to your mate in and out of the bedroom, there will be red-hot monogamy.

A SEXUAL GETAWAY

Sometime during these eight weeks, set aside at least 24 hours (we recommend 48 hours) to get away with the purpose of reconnection emotionally and sexually. If you have the opportunity for 48 hours, spend the first evening doing something fun (remember recreational intimacy from chapter 3?). Get a good night's sleep. If you are ready, you can also try one of the types of sexual exercises, but feel no pressure to do so. You have some time to decide when you'd like to connect. If you only have 24 hours, still enjoy some recreation, a little dinner, and then decide if you'd like to explore in the evening or wait until you have had a good night's rest. (You may decide to take turns giving: Tonight is hers, the morning is his.)

Prepare for the getaway. Bring all the comforts from home: your favorite lighting (candles, scarves to shade the lamps, little white Christmas lights), lotions and oils you enjoy, and either new comfortable loungewear and lingerie or favorites. You will want to also pack bathing suits (we suggest a hotel with pool and Jacuzzi, and if you can afford it, a Jacuzzi tub in your room). You might also want to bring comfort foods such as chocolate, strawberries, and a sparkling drink with crystal gasses. Consider tossing in a CD player with some favorite romantic tunes. (Bonus romantic points for downloading all your favorites to a CD or iPod for hours of continuous romantic music.) You can buy CDs that have romantic themes in most all music genres.

Also, prepare your heart by praying specifically for your spouse every day the week before the sexual escape. Ask God to help your mate feel encouraged, blessed, reenergized, and renewed. Pray that your love is rekindled and your sexual fascination rejuvenated.

Either before the getaway or after diner and emotional reconnection (you know you are there if you are both smiling), decide which sexual intimacy exercise you'd like to try first.

Four Kinds of Sexual Intimacy Exercises

Exploration

This exercise is to give you both ample relaxed time to explore each other's bodies and pleasures in a non-rushed environment. Keep in mind that the general atmosphere you are going for is trust, relaxation, and enjoyment. Before beginning this activity, do things together that make you laugh or smile. Laughter is one of the quickest ways to relax your body.

Sit in a Jacuzzi or take a shower or bubble bath together. If you'd like, ask him to massage your back before beginning this exercise. While completely undressed, as a husband, lie down on the bed, resting semi-propped up on pillows, and then invite your wife to place herself between your legs, resting back on your chest. Now, as the woman, guide your spouse in what pleasures you. Take a few deep relaxing breaths and then take your fingers (and his) and run them through your hair. Massage your scalp. Move along your face, neck, and then down your shoulders, arms, and fingertips. You can ask your spouse to stop and give more pleasure at any place (massage your shoulders or temples, or kiss any of the spots mentioned thus far). Now move down your shoulders toward your breasts. Show and tell him what pleasures you when he touches your breasts (feel free to change positions if you'd like him to kiss or suck or maneuver your breasts from another direction than the way he is sitting).

When you are ready (be in no hurry), encourage him to move down your abdomen, hips, and over to your thighs and legs, feet and toes, massaging, stroking, kissing, or whatever gives you pleasure. (Again, enjoy it and take your time—take all day!) When you are ready, move your mate's attention up the inner ankle, knee, and thigh into the pelvic region. (Now, husband, really take your time here. Explore, move so you can get a better look, kiss, stroke, etc. as your wife directs with words or most likely with moans and sighs soon.) See how long you can keep her pleased. As the wife, feel free to come to orgasm through his stroking with his fingers or from oral sex. Decide ahead of time if you'd like to consummate intercourse at this time, or if you want to switch places and delay intercourse until your spouse has also gone through having you please him slowly like this. (We actually suggest intercourse to complete this activity. Then eat some food, do a little exercise, and come back and have the husband take his turn and move to intercourse again. If you are more than 40, you might want to space out these exercises about 24 hours apart—or have some Viagra handy).

When you are ready to repeat the favor, place him between your legs. Some men might prefer to see you and have you explore from in front of him in full view. As you pleasure your mate, alternate time on the genital region with long outward strokes from his pelvic region. This will pay off as he will enjoy his orgasm more fully when he climaxes because all the nerve systems of his body have been "warmed up." Husband, feel free to kindly ask for your wants and desires, and tell her exactly when she is pleasuring you and when it intensifies. (Note to wife: This is not a time to be shy. Think of yourself as a scientist or a great explorer. You are seeking to gather important, vital information for a great and noble cause.)

Reconnection

If your schedule has just been insane and it has been a while since your last episode of red-hot monogamy, you'll want a sexual retreat that is spalike in its pace. (You might even consider going to a spa on day one. Or if you must travel to get there, go the morning of day two.)

Show up early at the spa, eat a light breakfast, and then work out together with a few classes or just some treadmill, stationary cycle, or walking. Swim, and then enjoy a nice, leisurely lunch poolside while you chat and get reconnected emotionally. You might decide on treatments such as a full-body massage, a facial, a manicure, or a pedicure. The husband might want to lie in the hammock and read the newspaper while his wife enjoys a haircut and makeover. By dinnertime you will be all dressed up and need a place to go. Plan ahead to enjoy a wonderful meal of your favorite foods and then afterward some dancing or a walk on the beach or other nearby romantic spot.

If you are up to it, take the remainder of the evening to explore a few new sensations: the touch of velvet, silk, a feather boa. Explore the sensation of various oils or lotions, try any of the many Red-Hot Romance Ideas, or simply try some sexual positions or techniques you usually don't have time for at home.

Arrange a late checkout so you can be sure to sleep in and have a nice leisurely breakfast, enjoy a stroll, and maybe have one last sexual encounter before you head home and back to reality. If you can, even after checking out of the hotel, have child care covered so you can enjoy a fun activity on the way home, dinner, and then home just in time to kiss the kids goodnight and fall into bed in each other's arms.

The goal of this getaway is to come home physically rested, emotionally connected, and sexually relieved. You want to return hopeful that life can look better than it has been. Now is not the time to bring up topics that are a bone of contention. Deal with those on a date the week following the getaway. The issues and problems won't seem nearly as bad when you are rested and connected.

Learning a New Skill

Sometimes even in a loving, caring, and committed marriage relationship, things in the sexual area are just not going smoothly. After a doctor's appointment and a counseling session (or more) to rule out any organic or mental health reasons for the issue, take some good information with you on the topic and go away to learn some new skills or coping mechanisms to deal with the issue. Often, when there is a biological cause, we still need some new skills to adjust to what nature is giving us as a couple to work with at the moment.

Some hurdles that might need a new learning curve are:

- Premature ejaculation
- Sexual anxiety
- Erectile dysfunction
- Vaginimus (pain in intercourse)
- Lack of sexual drive or inability to achieve orgasm

Less common, but ones that will definitely need extra TLC and education accompanied with tremendous understanding are:

- Sex after physical trauma (breast cancer, prostrate treatment, or any severe injury)
- Sex after emotional trauma (rape, loss of a child, or any emotional pain that causes grief or overwhelming emotional upheaval)

For the last two, or anytime you are trying to process emotional grief, a getaway to comfortable surroundings with absolutely no expectations will be a healing balm.

For the more commonplace obstacles, creating space and time to learn more about the issue and then taking the time to try techniques to compensate can rejuvenate your love life. Cliff and Joyce Penner have written many books detailing help in these areas (*Restoring the Pleasure* is most helpful), and *The Act of Marriage After 40* will help with ones common to older couples. In addition, taking good resources from the medical and psychological experts away with you and learning from them will give you information to enhance your love life.

Healing of an Emotional Wound

If there has been a breach of trust (addictions, affair), then intensive personal and couple counseling is in order. In our book *Love, Honor and Forgive*, we lay out Six Statements of Forgiveness and give couples the principles to wipe the slate clean and begin again.

Sexual obstacles are not limited to physical difficulties, however. Many people struggle in their sexual lives because of spiritual problems. We shared earlier in the book that Ephesians 5 clearly states that the love between a husband and wife is a picture of the love between Christ and His church. In other words, red-hot monogamy helps proclaim the gospel of Jesus Christ. Since the devil is opposed to the gospel, he is opposed to anything that helps people understand the gospel. This is one of the reasons sex is so abused in our world. There is a spiritual push to distort our understanding of human sexuality. Pornography, casual sex, and self-gratification are all glamorized in the fabric of our society. Our kids are inundated with it, our computers are flooded with it, and our thoughts are challenged by it. To put it simply, your sexuality is under attack spiritually.

To combat the assault, every couple should institute some simple measures to safeguard the love gift they have been given. At a bare minimum, you ought to be praying together. We know that some of you are uncomfortable praying together, and we very respectfully recommend that you try to push past this discomfort. You are willing to get naked and have sex together; surely you can pray together. There really is no secret to a successful prayer life as a couple. Keep it short, be yourself, and pray daily. Don't try to be overly spiritual, and don't imitate anyone else. God made you the way He wants you to be, so talk to Him the way you talk with the most important people in your life. Once you have practiced a few times, praying together will be natural to you.

In addition to prayer, reading the Bible together is extremely helpful in creating a safe zone in your marriage. Demons do not like the truth, and when you proclaim the truth aloud in your home, you create an environment that is irritating to them. This is exactly what Jesus did in Matthew 4 when He was led out to the wilderness to be tempted by the devil. He quoted the Bible over and over again. Your spiritual fortress will be further strengthened if you share with one another what God is teaching you. You can accomplish this by going through a devotional book together or doing your personal devotions separately and then taking time to share with one another in a relaxed setting what God is currently doing in your life.

The spiritual battle can be more intense than this if your past has been marked by decisions based on some deception. Each of these decisions opens up footholds from which Satan can have influence in your life. You may be more self-conscious than you know you ought to be. You may be unable to overcome a relatively simple habit. You may be run by guilt and shame, even though you know intellectually you are forgiven for everything. These can all be signs of a lack of spiritual freedom. If you suspect this may be your story, we encourage you to talk to your pastor to see if he is familiar with *Steps to Freedom in Christ* (www.freedom inchrist.com). If he is not, you can go to their website and find a trained associate in your area to lead you through the steps.

The toughest obstacles you face are in the area of emotional programming. You were born with an innate ability to trust your parents. Early in life, you believed everything they said and trusted everything they did. As a result, your early life experiences create emotional programming in life. In other words, your definition of intimate love is attached to whatever you experienced as a child, unless you do the hard work to rebuild your emotional definition of love. If you grew up in a balanced, encouraging home, you are wondering what we are talking about. You have a healthy perspective on love, and you naturally choose to be with people you can trust. If, on the other hand, you grew up in a chaotic home environment (by chaotic, we mean anything that doesn't fit with the way life was supposed to be), you will have a tendency to have low-quality relationships and you will unwittingly sabotage your success at relationships. It is common for those who have experienced relational trauma to be unreasonable, abusive, and unpredictable with the ones they love most.

While you are tearing down the relationship, you are internally telling yourself to stop talking this way and stop acting this way. You may have tried self-discipline and self-help books but have found they make no difference. If this is your experience, you must take it seriously. The path out of this destructive living is simple to outline but hard to accomplish. The path consists of aggressive forgiveness of those who have hurt you and strategic decisions that will reprogram the way you emotionally attach to others. It is the rare person who can do this on his or her own. We recommend you commit to a regimen of focused counseling followed by a deliberate routine of personal growth. If you don't connect with the first counselor you see, check out another one. Every counselor has a unique personality and specialty. Don't get frustrated. Just keep looking until you find one you connect with. If you need a starting point, go to New Life Ministries at www. newlife.com.

When your relationship is reestablished to the place you are feeling love toward one another and want to take the step to reconnect emotionally and sexually, below is a meaningful ritual to do at the foot of the bed before engaging in intercourse as it marks the moment of a fresh start.

Pray this verse over the spouse who has caused the pain:

_____ (name of spouse) has been crucified with Christ and _____ no longer lives, but

Christ lives in _____. The life _____ lives in the body, _____ lives by faith in the Son of God, who loved _____ and gave Himself for _____ (Galatians 2:20).

Have the spouse who caused the pain pray:

Hear my cry for mercy as I call to You for help, as I lift up my hands toward Your Most Holy Place (Psalm 28:2). Forgive [me], who [has] sinned against You; forgive all the offenses [I] have committed against You (1 Kings 8:50).

Pray this verse over the victim of the pain:

[Lord, You heal] the brokenhearted and bind up (_____) wounds (Psalm 147:3). Then Your light will break forth like the dawn, and Your healing will quickly appear (Isaiah 58:8) and provide for those who grieve...bestow on them a crown of beauty instead of ashes, the oil of gladness instead of mourning, and a garment of praise instead of a spirit of despair (Isaiah 61:3).

Pray this over the spouse who caused the pain:

If my [_____], who [is] called by [Your] name, will humble [himself or herself] and pray and seek [Your] face and turn from [his or her] wicked ways, then will [You] hear from heaven and will forgive [his or her] sin and will heal [our marriage] (2 Chronicles 7:14).

Then use your original wedding vows or the ones below, to renew your commitment:

Husband: I, _____, take you _____, to be my lawfully wedded wife, to have and to hold from this day forward. I promise to love you, comfort you,

honor you, and forsaking all others, cling only to you
as long as I live.

Wife: I,_____, take you _____, to be my
lawfully wedded husband, to have and to hold from
this day forward. I promise to love you, comfort you,
honor you, and forsaking all others, cling only to you
as long as I live.

When reestablishing the sexual relationship, we encourage the
spouse who caused the pain or breach to give the gift of making
the first sex act all about the spouse and full of the things that
first drew you together. By adding in the familiar territory, it is a
reminder that it was worth it to spend all the time and energy to re-
establish the relationship. At any time during the time of intimacy,
if the spouse who was hurt is hesitant or has an emotional reaction,
then the spouse who initially caused the trauma should be overly
patient, overly sensitive, and overly understanding. Forgiveness is
one thing. Reestablishing trust and a trusting sexual relationship is
another and takes time. Sometimes lots and lots of time.

(A note to the spouse who was hurt: Our friends Bob and
Audrey Misner have a powerful book on restoring love after an
affair, *Marriage Undercover*. While talking with them about their
story, Bob shared the wisdom that helped them turn the corner.
His mentor turned to Bob and said, "You have been hurt, but the
person who forgives has the power in the relationship." The forgiver
has the power to restore the relationship and to save the children
from the pain of divorce or an unhappy hostile environment. In
giving love as a symbol of forgiveness, you give yourself, your children, and your marriage the opportunity to build something even
better and stronger than it was before the pain because God will
add in His power as you replicate His grace, mercy, and love.)

WHERE IS THE LOVE?

Usually we encourage a change of location to add to the change of heart. But if you can't afford a getaway, then send the kids away for 48 hours. Spend the first evening talking about what you will look forward to and preparing for an enjoyable weekend: grocery shop together, change the sheets (if you can afford it, buy satin ones or flannel—change up some of your environment). Clean, cook, light candles, get ready for delighting one another. (By somehow sharing the responsibility, neither of you will feel resentful of having to do "all the work." You might use some money for the little extras: steak or scallops, new candles, new sheets, fresh flowers, etc.) The location of your bodies isn't as important as the location of your hearts. Enter the getaway with the sense that God's hand of favor and love is on you as a couple—because it is!

Hands-on Homework

*I*n your lovemaking together, you will experience some magical moments of red-hot monogamy. Now is the time to extend the magic as long as possible. Become masters of "the afterglow." After intercourse, extend the pleasure:

- Have him stay inside of you until he naturally relaxes so much he slips out. Stay intertwined.

- Pray and thank God aloud for each other while still interconnected and entwined. Stroke and caress your mate as you thank God for him or her.

- Prepare the recovery items and place them close to the bedside: bottles of cooled water and towels.

- Cozy up and spoon. Fall asleep in each other's arms.

- Express verbal thanks soon after—then all through the next day or two. Whisper reminders, leave notes, or send small trinkets that say "Thank you. It was wonderful, incredible, amazing, and I long for more."

- Continue to stroke and massage your mate. Scratch his back as he dozes off, or men, give an extra gift and bring her to orgasm a second time without intercourse.

- Slide off the top to the side but still touch. Look for a "comfort touch," a place he or she likes to be touched or held after sex before drifting off to relaxed sleep.

Red-Hot
ROMANCE IDEAS

151. Make your own fireworks on July Fourth. Buy red, white, or blue pj's for a midnight picnic in your room.

152. On Mother's Day and Father's Day, practice what made you a mom and dad. Have sex the way you did when one of your children was conceived. (Can you remember?)

153. On every January 1, renew your wedding vows privately at the foot of your bed, or pick a new place to renew every year and make it a romantic getaway to look forward to after the hustle and bustle of Christmas.

154. Make it a tradition to buy each other new Christmas pajamas or lingerie, and after you have all the kids in bed and their gifts out, enjoy unwrapping each other under the lights of the tree (if you have curious kiddos, you might want to put up your own tree behind a locked door or they are going to see more than "Mommy kissing Santa" under the mistletoe).

155. Find a cultural day to celebrate in style each year. For example, on Saint Patrick's Day, buy some dime-store shamrock stickers and all day slip your hand onto various private spots on your mate. At the end of the day, undress each other and see who has the most shamrocks of love decorating his or her body.

156. Create a brochure on your computer that looks like brochures sent out by romantic resorts. Personalize your brochure with your mate's name and include (or make) a

gift certificate (one you've already paid for) for a weekend or vacation away. But be careful. Our friend Ken was so great at his graphic design that his wife thought his brochure was just another one of those time-share ads. He had to fish it out of the trash and bring it back to her, saying, "Honey, really, I think you should read this!"

157. Black velvet in the middle of the night or a silk scarf or nightie might provide sex on the softer side.

158. Let sultry summer nights and your red-hot monogamy melt not just your heart, but some ice. Slide an ice cube over the fired-up body of your lover. Start in least sensitive areas, such as the arms and back, and move toward more intimate places. (Some people we've heard of also like the warmth of hot wax—but that just sounds painful to us! Maybe some lotion warmed up in your hands or run under the faucet.)

159. Blow in your spouse's ear or neck or on their genitals as you kiss. Your warm breath opens up blood vessels and causes blood to flow more freely.

160. If you are usually gentle and laid back in sex, step up and fire up and get a little primal fury going. Be more aggressive in your kisses and style. (But don't hurt anyone! Especially yourself if you are not in shape for such vigorous activity.)

161. You're a star! Create a date where your spouse is the center of attention. Have your mate get dressed to the nines. Find a place (a home or restaurant) where you can roll out the red carpet. Recruit some friends to be the paparazzi snapping pictures and others to be fans asking for autographs. Eat on white linen and china with crystal, and make sure

the waiter has on a tux and a white towel over his arm (your kids will get a kick out of playing these roles). Have something flaming for dessert.

162. Back to nature. Sit and watch fireflies or go to the beach and watch the waves roll in and out. Or simply sit on a country road and listen to the sounds of nature under a starlit sky.

163. Get your kicks on Route 66. Or travel some other famous highway: Highway 101 runs down the California coast, and there are beautiful winding roads through the Blue Ridge Mountains and Shenandoah Valley. Try to find the most picturesque place near your hometown.

164. Bike from one bed-and-breakfast to another. Some areas of the country, such as California's wine country and Vermont, have B-and-B's close together, so pick up a B-and-B book at the local library and chart your bike path.

165. Magic Genie. Find an old lantern, hand it to your mate, and tell them, "Tonight I will grant you any three wishes" (you might want to give a dollar limit). Or take turns granting each other three free sexual wishes.

166. Find a swimming hole. Create a rope swing or simply jump from a tree limb (feet first after checking the depth). Make sure before you leave your clothes hanging on the bushes that you have the spot to yourselves.

167. The Riddler. Give clues or rhymes that describe what you have planned for a date or an evening in bed. Make him or her guess the answers. Give your mate one clue at a time.

168. A different kind of scrabble. Grab just the tiles from the Scrabble game and each take ten or twelve at a time. Agree that your mate will do for you or to you whatever you can spell.

169. Class act. Take an interesting class together: art, literature, cooking, theology, or exercise.

170. Test your love. Get to know your mate. Personality tests can be fun and conversation starters. Check out www. classervices.com or *The Five Love Languages* by Gary Chapman. Then talk about what you learned about your mate that makes you appreciate him or her more.

171. Do a wish list date. Pick a theme (ideas for our bedroom decor, things I'd love to see your wear, how to make our home more like a hideaway) and then flip through magazines together and snip and clip the ideas for a file. This also gives you an idea file for presents.

172. Do a "count our many blessings" evening. Each of you take turns recounting the best days you can remember, things you are thankful for in your mate or family, and what you are grateful to God about. This is a nice pillow talk activity as it often can take a rough day and turn it into one that makes you more in the mood for intimacy.

173. Take a simple jigsaw puzzle, and on the back of about a third of the puzzle pieces, write something your mate can do for you. Turn all the puzzle pieces face up, and as you find the place they go, before putting them in place, check the back. This can be a way to fan the play on foreplay over a few days.

174. Attend a concert , symphony, or jazz fest. Play a little foot-
     sies or sing along to songs that have lyrics you and your
     mate might want to live out.

175. It's magic. Do magic tricks for your mate, and if he or she
     can't figure out how you did the trick, they must allow you
     to make a piece of their clothing "magically disappear."

8

Browsing in the Wonder of Each Other

WHAT TURNS ON A MAN AND WHAT TURNS ON A WOMAN

It was a surprise. Over dinner one night, in casual conversation, Bill said he was going to have to go to a convention for work. My heart sank. *Away again*, I thought. Just thinking it made me miss him. I felt as though I was always having to share him. He noticed the change in my countenance, and he leaned over to stroke my hair reassuringly as he said, "It's only a few days." I nodded knowingly and yet still said, "It's just that we get so little time alone."

The next morning, after I knew Bill had left the house for work and started his day's appointments, I called his office. I can't remember just what I said to get the information, but I acquired the name of the hotel where he would be staying for the convention. Then I made a call and begged a friend to come stay with the kids.

The day was a flurry. I wanted to use all five senses to create an affair to remember. I packed a picnic basket with candles, chocolate, two glasses, and a bottle of sparkling drink that had a big bow on it. I remember it well because the bow covered the very small thing I packed to wear later that night. I grabbed a portable stereo and bought a new Kenny G cassette. *He loves jazz,* I wistfully recalled. I threw in my makeup bag and a toothbrush.

On the way out of town I stopped at the mall. *A new outfit. A night like this needs a new outfit. Something he'll remember. Something that will stop him in his tracks and make him smile at me with that look—that look that makes me melt. It has to be soft.* I longed for his touch.

Back in the car, I listened to love songs on the radio. The station seemed to play all the songs we'd ever danced to—or sang to each other in whispered tones under soft lights. I found that I was leaning more and more forward in my seat, as if my heart was being drawn to him. The lights from the oncoming cars on the freeway seemed to dance and flicker. It was probably just a normal commute to most, but not to me. Tonight was going to be special—a secret rendezvous, a liaison. My heart raced as the odometer clicked down the miles. As I turned on the exit ramp, I felt my heart pounding, my desire for him was becoming so strong I thought I could hear my own heart beat—just as I had heard his so often after we'd been together intimately. I loved to lie quietly in his arms and rest my head on his chest. I breathed deeply and felt as if I could smell the deliciously familiar fragrance of his aftershave.

I parked the car discreetly behind a nearby business. His business partners and associates were also at this conference, and I couldn't take any chances at being seen or having my car recognized. I looked at my watch and sighed in relief. I had timed it just right. They would all still be out at the banquet, so I'd have time to sneak into his room undetected.

I must have seemed flustered when I asked for the room number and the key because the desk clerk mumbled, "Oh, I'm sorry, ma'am, the register only has one person registered for that room." A little panicked, I managed to pull myself together and answered as confidently as I could, "Oh, I'm his wife, and he wasn't sure if I'd be able to get off work to come." He nodded his head as though he believed me and handed me the key.

I walked quickly across the parking lot, my heart full of the thoughts of a woman in love. Again, I glanced at my watch. *I'll have to hurry to get everything set up. I want the atmosphere just right when he steps into the room.*

And it was just right. Soft flickering candlelight skipped across the ceiling to the mellow sound of a smooth saxophone as Bill stepped into the room. He saw me standing there in the shadows. He stared at me in stunned amazement. I knew at that moment I had recaptured his heart. As I ran to him, he wrapped his arms around me, twirled me around, and whispered, "Wow! What a surprise. I'm so glad you've come." Then we kissed and danced and did all the things I had dreamed we'd do. Finally, we fell asleep in each other's arms. My long blond hair fell across his chest, and it all felt so good—so right—and I could hear the beat of his heart as I lay there.

The quiet beeping of my watch alarm was an unwelcome sound the next morning. I knew I had to go, but I didn't want to. *Why can't these moments last forever?* I quietly slipped into my clothes and gathered up the staples of romance I had brought with me. I ran my fingers through his hair and we kissed. He thanked me again for coming, and he smiled that smile as I closed the door behind me. As I drove out of the parking lot, the sun was peeking up from its slumber and a hint of sunlight spilled across the steering wheel. It caught the corner of one of the facets of my diamond ring—the ring my husband had given me years before. I smiled. *No guilt,* I thought. *Just an affair to remember. An affair with my beloved husband.*

Your love will be memorable if you consider what turns on a man and what ignites the heart of a woman. Men and women have a different perspective on sex, and nothing can be done to alter that. Men are more aggressive in their approach to sexual activity and would love it if their wives were more adventurous in their intimate encounters. Women are more relational in their approach to sex and would like their husbands to slow down and be more understanding of their emotional needs. This tension exists because husbands and wives are wired differently by their Creator for sexual pleasure.

SEXUAL PRESSURE—A MAN'S JOURNEY

It has been said that sex is all men think about. This may be more true than any of us want to admit, but it doesn't mean that all men are warped in their sexual activity. Sex is a different pursuit for men than women because of the way they are made. The simplest way I know to understand a man's sex drive revolves around our concept that men are like waffles. The issues of a man's life are separated into boxes, and the center box of his waffle is the sex box. It is bigger than any of the others and can be entered from any other box. The reason this box is bigger is that it is subdivided into other boxes. Because most men are focused on sex much more than most women, it might be easy to conclude that they have a single-minded approach to sexual activity. But in reality, three independent forces drive a man's desire: a reproductive mandate, sexual tension, and a desire for intimacy.

A Reproductive Mandate

God created mankind for survival. To ensure our success, God built into the human species characteristics that consistently encourage sexual activity. In the case of men, God gave them an adventurous love for their wives. The very first marriage began as an adventure between God and Adam. Adam had named all the animals, looking for a suitable helpmate. When it was obvious that none existed, God put Adam to sleep, took a rib from his abdomen, and fashioned Eve. When Adam woke, boy, was he surprised! Standing before him was a perfect helpmate with stunning good looks. Adam was so taken by her appearance that he spontaneously broke out in song: "This is now bone of my bones and flesh of my flesh; she shall be called 'woman,' for she was taken out of man" (Genesis 2:23).

"God saw all that he had made, and it was very good" (Genesis 1:31). The original plan was to give each man eyes to admire his wife throughout their life together. The intensity of a man's ability to "notice" women was given to him so his wife would be attractive to him all the days of his life.

To say the least, this ability of a man to be captivated by his wife has been vastly exploited over the years. The beauty industry has put incredible pressure on women to always look fantastic. As a man sees more and more artificially beautiful women, he may lose his appreciation for the natural beauty of his wife. His sexual eyes were intended to allow his wife to go through the natural changes that age and motherhood bring without her becoming unappealing to him. She would continue to look great to him because he could feast his eyes on her. The modern media has turned his concentration into a commodity. As a result, any man who wants to have a lifelong relationship of pleasure with his wife must discipline his eyes to stay focused on her.

One of the ways he does this is to dream of new adventures with his wife. Sol and Sunny made love in their bedroom and in the garden. They loved each other at night and during the day. They loved each other with compliments and kisses all over their bodies. They chased each other, called out to each other, and caressed each other. They made love in conventional ways, and they experimented with creative ways of expressing their love.

Let me share just one example of how God calls men to adventure. In Genesis 12, God called out to Abraham to initiate the formation of the nation of Israel. Abraham was a conscientious man with a busy career, a wife, and family responsibilities that extended to his father and his nephew. In the middle of this focused life, God said to him, "Leave your country, your people and your father's household and go to the land I will show you" (Genesis 12:1). I have always been proud of Abraham, but I would hate to have to go home and tell my wife about this conversation.

"Sarai, we need to pack everything up. We are moving!"

"Really, Abe. Where are we moving to?"

"I don't know."

"What do you mean, you don't know?"

"God told me to leave our country, but He didn't say where we were going."

"Let me get this right. God told you to leave, but He never said where?"

"Yep, that's about it. Isn't it great that God would talk directly to me and show me His will?"

"Are you sure it was God? This does not sound like something God would ask me to do!"

I can only imagine that Abraham got *the look*. You know the one I am talking about. It is that look that only a woman can give and, when she does, the temperature in the room lowers a few degrees. My (Bill's) theory is that it was attached to the rib. That is why only women can successfully give *the look*.

Despite Sarai's hesitation, Abraham really was called by God to an adventurous pursuit. A man is at his best when he has some adventure to pursue, and this extends to his relationship with his wife. Each man's adventure is personal and reflects his approach to life. It does not always involve rugged activities. It can be intellectual, organizational, or musical. It can be physical, spiritual, or relational. The key is that the adventure takes a man to the end of his ability so he has to cry out to God for His grace and strength.

This applies to our sexual life in that we want to experience a progressive relationship with our wives. When sex becomes routine, it dulls in its appeal. When there is no variety, we begin to view it as a responsibility rather than a gift. When our wives look for ways to extend the adventure in our sexual experience, we fall in love over and over again.

Sexual Tension

The second force has to do more with stress than intimacy. Following ejaculation, semen begins to build up in a man's body, creating a sense of physical pressure. When a man becomes sexually active, his body adjusts to an anticipated schedule of intercourse. For example, if a husband and wife start off their relationship enjoying sexual pleasure every couple days, his body will prepare to ejaculate on that schedule. But no couple ever stays "on schedule," and that is where the tension builds. His body still prepares to release the semen even if he knows intellectually it is unreasonable.

For most men, this is where the tyranny of sex shows up. When he is not able to ejaculate on schedule, he experiences a number of physiological and emotional reactions. The feeling of pressure in his groin area becomes a nagging reminder. He finds himself staring at his wife more as her features intensify in his mind. He longs to be with her as her features look more attractive to him. As time goes by, he then becomes irritable, even unreasonable. He loses sight of much of what is great about life. Music seems dull, sunsets are distractions, conversation is painful, and all other tasks become either boring or overwhelming. The whole time he is saying to himself, "Get a grip. You are stronger than this. It won't hurt to wait." But no amount of reasoning with himself reduces the tension he feels in his body.

This struggle is intensified even more if stress is high in life. The process of orgasm for a man is so intense and easy to achieve that it is his preferred method for stress relief. As general stress increases in a man's life, his awareness of the tension in his body is heightened. The release of semen at ejaculation not only relieves the tension in his body, it also transports him mentally and emotionally into the box of sexual expression. When he enters that box, all the cares of his life are put on hold. The fact that good sex is usually followed by sleep only adds to the impact that sexual activity has in relieving stress in his life.

I believe that most men would like to have more control over this part of their sex drive. It just will not let up even though he would love to find the off switch. The tension builds involuntarily and consumes much more of his life than he is comfortable with. He also has no idea how to explain this to his wife. He doesn't want her to think he lacks self-control, or worse, that he has a perverted outlook on sex. He also doesn't want to put undue pressure on her, but he can't stop the process going on inside himself. Every man longs for his wife to accept the intensity of this compartment because he is bound to live with it. When she is sensitive and compassionate about the constant intensity of his sex drive, he is amazed and grows in his love for her. When she is critical of it or insensitive, he turns inward and silently fights the struggle alone.

A Desire for Intimacy

The third compartment of a man's sex box is the one that women find most attractive. A man does not love sex just because of what it does for him physically, he also longs to be significantly connected to the love of his life. He wants to know his wife and be known by her. He longs for the safe haven of a loving marriage the way she does. The difference is that a man visits this box while his wife weaves intimacy into the fabric of her life. When a man is in the intimacy box, he is attentive to his wife's needs, he is sensitive to her emotions, and he is a patient listener. The only disappointment for his wife is that he usually doesn't spend as much time here as she would like.

The Sexual Dance—A Woman's Waltz

Men, your wife's view of sex is much different than yours. Her sexual fulfillment is connected to everything else in her life. When she feels close to you emotionally, she is more responsive. When she is in touch with her children and is proud of how you father them, she is more attracted to you. When her career is moving forward and you are supportive of her pursuits, she finds you irresistible. The more you are a part of her life, the stronger is her desire for you.

In addition, her sexual experience revolves around her menstrual period. Every month she is reminded of her reproductive potential. As a man, you would probably like to think that her constant interaction with her reproductive process would make her more interested in sex. But much of her menstrual cycle is uncomfortable and inconvenient. She has no choice but to experience this cycle every month. Some days she feels very sexy and interested in intimate contact with you. On other days she is out of sorts, even though she may try not to be.

PMS—Myth or Monster?

Four different hormones are involved in a woman's reproductive cycle, influencing her behavior and how she feels at different times of the month. Almost all doctors accept that a significant number of women suffer regularly from a variety of physical ailments commonly called Premenstrual syndrome (PMS). According to a pamphlet recently published by Women's Health Concern, PMS has six major physical symptoms and ten mental ones. Among these are irritability, depression, anxiety, hostility, headache, and backache, as well as unusually painful menstruation. It is hard to feel sexy when you are battling these challenges. But the pamphlet acknowledges that most sufferers will experience no more than three of them during any one cycle.

A Fascinating Dynamic

The news on PMS may be discouraging, but there is a remarkable benefit to the way in which a woman is created. It may take more for her to reach arousal, but when things are right, she can experience pleasure much longer and more intensely than her husband. The big difference between male and female orgasm is that a woman does not necessarily need to recover from one orgasm before she can have another. Many women frequently experience two or more orgasms in a row without descending from the plateau phase of sexual arousal. It is very possible that most women can experience multiple orgasms but do not do so for lack of experimentation or because of psychological or social inhibition.

It is obvious from the female anatomy that God intended that sexual pleasure would be a normal part of a woman's life. Her breasts are impossible to hide and draw her husband's attention to her on a daily basis. Though small, the clitoris contains as many nerve endings as a penis, and its only purpose is to provide sexual pleasure. When a man commits himself to his wife's sexual fulfillment, a fascinating dynamic takes place. She will experience orgasms more often and may enjoy multiple orgasms on many occasions. He, on the other hand, will have his ego boosted because he feels like a better lover with each orgasm she experiences.

HOW TO KEEP HER
COMING BACK FOR MORE

The greatest way you can show your spouse you value his or her sexuality is by committing yourself to learning how to give pleasure rather than take it. Our friends Jim and Sally Conway, authors of *Traits of a Lasting Marriage*, like to describe the differences between men's and women's sexual response this way: Women respond like an electric stove. You push the button to turn on the burner, and at first there is no immediate response. Yet slowly the burner warms up until it is red-hot. When you turn the burner off, it continues to be red-hot and then slowly cools back down. Men, on the other hand, respond like a gas burner—instant on, instant off.

Women become very encouraging to their husbands when they work through their inhibitions and open themselves up to trying new things sexually, but the art of lovemaking is a little different for men. To get your wife's body to respond in sexual ecstasy, you need to touch her heart. God wired her in such a way that she brings everything in her life to bed with her. When you deliver the message that you care about everything in her world, she develops an insatiable desire for you. The risk a man is challenged to take is a curiosity risk. Your wife has many layers that either hinder or enhance her sexual experience. A great lover is committed to working through these layers. Women are naturally self-conscious, so compliments are vital to foreplay. A risk-taking husband is consistently looking for ways to help his wife appreciate her beauty. Many a man grows tired of his wife's constant need to hear how beautiful, talented, and valuable she is. He wishes she could just believe what he has been saying. He wishes she could process life more like a man while she continues to look like a woman. But she is a woman, through and through. She constantly processes life, so the landscape of her experience is constantly changing. Her evaluation of herself rapidly adjusts with every new thing she hears or sees or reads.

Orgasm for a woman is an involuntary response, much like a sneeze. You cannot make yourself have an orgasm; rather, you can make choices that stimulate your body's desire for orgasmic release. The most vital elements are pent-up sexual energy; a relaxed and secure environment; and the privacy and freedom to express (loudly if necessary), your feelings in moans, purrs, and groans.

The big three challenges for a husband are to compliment her, listen to her, and romance her.

Compliment Her

Your compliments raise her confidence level. At times she feels pretty but her body is constantly changing, so she has a hard time holding on to her sense of beauty. When she becomes convinced that your opinion of her is stable, even though her opinion of herself is wavering, your love becomes a safe place.

I (Bill) am amazed at how Pam has clung to certain things I have said throughout our years together. Early in our marriage I asked her if I could call her "Angel." She asked me why, and I told her, "I want to call you Angel because you have made my life better than it could have been on my own. Much of what I am now doing, I would never have even thought about without you." When I noticed what a big difference this statement made in Pam's countenance, I was very proud of myself, but there is a risk in coming up with great compliments. I had now proven to Pam that I have the ability to compliment my way right into her heart. Since she now knows I have this skill, she expects me to use it on a regular basis. As a result, if I have not called her "Angel" recently, I begin to hear statements such as, "So, you don't think I am all that valuable, do you? I am not sure you really care anymore. I think you just take me for granted." The risk I must take is accepting that one good compliment requires another...and another...and another...

Listen to Her

The second challenge to unlocking your wife's passion is listening. As we have said, she is wired to process life continually. She doesn't take breaks in the action the way we men do. She knows this deluge of thoughts and emotions are complicated, but she has been this way her whole life. She cannot turn the thought process off, and she desperately hopes the complex layers of her experience do not turn you off. When you take time to listen to her, she has an opportunity to put her inner stirring in order. As she connects all these experiences to you, there is a complete investment of her heart in you. You become the safe place in her life where she can let herself go. I still remember the first time I really learned how to listen to Pam by staying curious about her. I could tell it was one of the most enjoyable things she had ever experienced. She told me later she felt like the most interesting person in the world simply because I was listening. There was no challenge that night discovering red-hot monogamy. Then reality set in. I had proved I could do this, so I was going to have to be good at this for the rest of my life.

Romance Her

The third of the big three challenges is romance. Every time you romance your wife, you deliver the message that she is important. When you give her flowers, you tell her she was worth the effort. When you buy her a gift, you tell her she is worth the money. When you take her on a date, you tell her she is worth the investment. Because her thoughts about herself are always moving, romance helps her remember that she is valuable and worthwhile. Everything in her life is competing for her attention, and romance keeps you in first place.

One man called into our radio program with a story that proves it is the thought that counts. It was March in upper Minnesota. His wife had cabin fever, but there was no money for a Florida cruise. So he invited his wife on a picnic. Her response was, "A picnic? There's a blizzard outside!" Then he led her down to the basement, where he had placed Astroturf, fake flowers, the kids' wading pool, and even a plastic yard deer. Among all this he had put down a plaid picnic blanket and a scrumptious picnic of her favorite foods. He had even taken the time to find a recording of forest sounds (birds chirping, babbling brook). They had an afternoon of red-hot monogamy in a "mountain meadow."

Though every woman is different in what she thinks is romantic, anything that makes a connection to her heart will do. As a result, every husband who wants to be romantic must become a student of his wife. He needs to be willing to take risks and evaluate how well each one worked. That is why we have included Red-Hot Romance Ideas throughout this book. Some of them will work well with your wife, while some of them will be a flop, because your wife has her own romantic quotient. The challenge for you is to keep trying romantic gestures until you discover what works best with the love of your life.

HOW TO KEEP HIM COMING BACK FOR MORE

While most men are the ones pushing their wives to the edge of the sexual envelope, at times we all hit a slump when sex feels like a rut. You may be avoiding intimacy because inside you feel *If I have to do this same old, same old pattern one more time, I am going to lose my mind!* If that is true, you need to talk, outside the bedroom, about your feelings and perhaps share an idea or two. It is best to not hold these ideas up as an expectation, but rather as ideas to be accepted or declined. Or even better, go out of your way to do something in bed you know pleases her, and as you reach out, she may follow your lead and step a bit further over her comfort line as she naturally is swept up in the moment and allows her passion to carry her.

This is the time to take small steps to change up the batting order. Just a note here though, ladies. If a man verbally asks for something in the area of sexuality, he has most likely stewed on it for some time. Before you shoot him and his request down, at least offer to pray about it. Try not to bruise his ego when he talks to you about these kinds of intimate things. You can respond with a simple, "Let me think about that one, will you? I like thinking about you, so I want to daydream and rotate this over in my mind first." Men, the request might not get a complete green light, but she might be willing to meet you partway or offer another, just as exciting idea that she is more comfortable with. The point is to take the risk of talking about your sexual experience and see what develops.

To me, the easiest way to become a risk taker is to focus on Bill during sex. I ask myself things like, "I wonder how he'll feel if I touch him here?" "I wonder how he'll respond if I whisper this?" Or I simply start praying. *Wow, God, it sure is a privilege to be married to such a great man. I can't believe You trusted me with the awesome, amazing responsibility of Bill's pleasure and fulfillment. I am the only woman in the world who has this right before You.* When I notice that Bill is tired (or preoccupied or discouraged—whatever I sense) from the stress of life, I ask God for His insight. *God, give me the wisdom to know what to do to sexually please him, to comfort him, to encourage him, to give him power and confidence, and to help him feel cherished and loved and mighty!* As I pray, ideas and actions just spontaneously begin to happen. I believe God smiles on us when we truly are seeking to be the "helpmate" He designed us to be way back in the Garden of

Eden. And remember, before the fall, Adam and Eve were "naked and not ashamed," so Eve started out as a sexual risk taker.

I Just Don't Feel Like It

If I (Pam) have heard it once, I have heard it a thousand times. I recognize the pain in her eyes before she even says a word. Then, with her head hanging, and a whisper in her voice, she begins. "Can I talk to you? Uh, ummm, it's kind of personal. See, I have this great husband. He is a nice guy, but I just can't, I just don't...feel like sex anymore. If I never had it again, I would be fine...but that's not fair to my sweet husband. What can I do? What's wrong with me? I mean, I used to like sex..."

Well, to start with, let's get rid of the guilt and shame. What you are going through is normal. Most women at some point aren't up for sex. However, if your libido wanes for more than six to eight weeks, you should consider taking steps to discover why. If it has been months and you find yourself purposefully finding excuses, such as working on projects with the kids late at night so you don't have to go to bed or faking a headache, cramps, and so on, you should seek help—and not just for your spouse, but for you. Sex is God's gift to you as well.

In 1999 an American Medical Association report said that up to 43 percent of women experience female sexual dysfunction (FSD). FSD is defined as a lack of interest in sex, lack of genital lubrication or sensitivity, inability to have orgasm, or pain during intercourse. At the Female Sexual Medicine Center at UCLA, urologist Jennifer Berman, MD, and her sister, psychotherapist Laura Berman, PhD, are exploring FSD from a medical stand-point.

A patient can come in for an entire sexual workup, which includes questions to find out your overall feelings and thoughts and beliefs about your body image and sex; a psychological session to look for emotional red flags (such as being depressed, acutely stressed, addicted to pornography, self-critical, sexual or emotional abuse, addicted to drugs or alcohol, guilt over early sexual encounters, or shame from carrying an STD); and a game plan for needed therapy. "We look at your problem as one big puzzle," said Laura. "We try to identify all the pieces potentially contributing to the picture."[1]

After ruling out mental and emotional issues, a physical checkup is given to discern if there are abnormalities (nerve damage, side effects of antidepressants or other medications, or from ailments such as high blood pressure or vaginal infection). A reading is taken of blood flow levels in the clitoris, labia, and vagina. Another probe, a biothesiometer, checks the sensitivity of nerves to heat, cold, and vibration. Blood tests are taken to rule out certain diseases and check hormone levels. (Lower testosterone levels in either a man or woman will lower the sex drive.)

A woman can patch together her own à la carte method of self-care to regain or experience desire and move toward the ability to experience orgasm. Ask for blood work at your doctor's or take a saliva test from a place like Life Wellness Pharmacy. A regular OB/GYN exam by a doctor familiar with FSD along with Kegel exercises should start you on the right track. And, of course, if you have experienced any sexual trauma, counseling is also in order.

The Mighty Kegel!

There is a machine called a "Fria" (which you can buy for just over $100) that measures pelvic floor strength and guides you through exercises to strengthen it. Or you can do a few simple exercises daily to strengthen your pubococcygeus muscle (PC) that will richly enhance your sex life and help you to become more orgasmic. Beverly Whipple, coauthor of *The G Spot*, says, "The stronger the PC muscle...the greater a woman's orgasmic response." The easiest way to find your PC muscle is the next time you urinate, stop the urine stream and then start it again. You have just contracted your PC. Doing PC push-ups is wise because it will enhance your ability to experience orgasm and your mate's sexual experience as well.

Your goal is to lift your pelvic floor up and in. Try to contract it ten times three times a day and work your way up to 50 times each session. The great thing about these Kegel exercises (named after the doctor who developed them) is that you can do them while driving, sitting at the computer, doing dishes, or watching TV. No one knows or can tell, unless you practice them while having sex, which we highly recommend as it will enhance the experience! The upside of doing Kegel push-ups is that will help you get in the mood!

THE TASTE OF YOU

We are not sure why the topic of oral sex has been so controversial. Remember our sample couple, Sunny and Sol? It seems they enjoyed kissing all over the body:

His fruit is sweet to my taste (Song of Songs 2:3).

Let my lover come into his garden and taste its choice fruits (4:16). (The garden is a metaphor for genitals.)

I have come into my garden...I have eaten my honey-comb...drink your fill, O lovers (5:1).

My lover has gone down to his garden, to the bed of spices, to browse in the gardens...he browses among the lilies (6:2-3). (To browse means he is taking his time to be focused on her genitals. In 5:1, the term used is "eat," denoting a mouth-to-genital connection that is unrushed.)

I would give you spiced wine to drink, the nectar of my pomegranates (8:2). (Again, you drink with your lips, and the pomegranate is another term for garden/genitals.)

Kissing is kissing. Is it more spiritual and acceptable to kiss the lips, the elbow, the knee, the breast, or the genitals? All the body is given as a gift to your spouse in 1 Corinthians 7:4 (your body is not your own but your mate's). With an entire book of the Bible dedicated to marital, sexual love, God could have specified any part of the body that was off limits, but conspicuously, He didn't.

Overall, about 50 percent of Christian couples surveyed by Dr. Tim LaHaye and his wife, Beverly, said they engaged in oral sex. When they surveyed Christian doctors, 73 percent found nothing wrong with the practice of oral sex for a Christian. And 77 percent of pastors felt oral sex was acceptable. Some theologians struggle with oral sex as not being "natural." They argue that the mouth is not being used for its intended purpose. However, nowhere in the Bible does it say the mouth was not made for this reason, and the mouth is used to kiss genitals in the Song of Songs. The Penners say, "Many people use moral arguments… to defend against an activity that is personally uncomfortable for them…and keep them from dealing with the real issues of personal emotional conflict or discomfort."[2]

Some might not have moral questions, but they do wonder if oral sex is clean. There are actually more germs in your mouth than in the genitalia region, so if you take a shower, bath, or a swim, you'll find things plenty clean to be attractive. Maybe it's a matter of overcoming a mental wall you have about the secretions. Simply ask yourself, "Do I love my mate through and through—body, soul, and spirit?" If you can focus on loving *everything* about your mate, the details will fall into place.

So if it seems to be acceptable, how do you make it enjoyable?

Never force it. You can ask for oral sex, like anything else in the area of sexuality, but it should never be an expectation or demand. Out of love, go with the conservative partner until your spouse initiates or gives the green light for a new sexual experience. In the same way, out of love, the more conservative partner might pray about being open to trying new experiences.

Learn it. Get a few basics down. To please a man, focus your tongue on the head of the penis at the little *v* you see. Kissing, licking, and sucking will send your man into orbit. You will discover exactly what pleases him if you ask for directions. (Treat it like an eye appointment. Do you like this? Or this?) Most men, if they are honest, would love it if, at least on occasion, a wife would experiment with oral sex. Plenty of men fantasize about having their wife bring them to full climax in this manner. It can be a little work to give this gift, and if you are afraid of the ejaculation, you can have a towel nearby to catch the semen. However, given the verses about "wine" and "drinking your fill," one can at least wonder if this biblical couple enjoyed bringing each other to climax and actually enjoyed the fluids that accompany this sacrificial other-focused act.

Whether you bring him to climax orally or not, there are a few other pleasure spots to be aware of. The space between his anus and the base of his scrotum; along the shank of his penis and his testicles. Cupping, caressing, kissing, sucking, licking, or rubbing these parts with any of your body parts will produce pleasure.

To please a woman, take a patient approach. With a touch as light as a feather, and a slow hand (or with almost all kisses), start with less sensitive areas, such as her face, neck, shoulders, tummy, and thighs. When you have her attention, work your way inward toward her labia and vagina. Remember, the goal in loving a woman is to reach her heart through her body. By taking time, showing interest in every part of her body, you are giving her the message "You are beautiful. You are exciting. You are amazing."

As this message sinks in, she becomes more and more aroused. The way to make sure this message arrives in all its glory, slowly work toward her clitoris. There are more nerve endings here than any other place in her body. It actually appears that the only purpose for the clitoris is to stimulate your wife sexually. If that is the case, this is a part of her body you want to get well acquainted with. Your job is to bring her sexual energy in from her extremies toward her genitalia. Picture her body like a waterfall. The water must flow down and over all the folds and curves to gather in the lowest spot and pool up. You'll want it to pool up in her G-spot. Keep your hands busy touching and caressing, even while your lips are concentrating on kissing.

Circle around her clitoris, readying it for more direct stroking. Here is when the choice comes. You can continue to hand stroke with well manicured finger tips, or you can switch to oral sex/ foreplay at this point.

Either way, the place you are aiming to discover is her G-spot. It is located about two inches up her vagina on the upper wall (if she is lying on her back). As you stimulate these regions (clitoris and G-spot), the places that give her pleasure will engorge and self-lubricate, making your job even easier. If you can continue to stimulate both the G-spot and the clitoris, and she trusts you emotionally, she will have the opportunity to experience an explosive orgasm. If you add in pleasuring a woman's breasts as you are pleasuring her orally in her genital region, it is like a triangle of pleasure that will intensify her enjoyment.

Practice it. Like any technique in lovemaking, the more you do it, the more you will be able to please your spouse.

The Power of Words

More mighty than the Kegel, more magnificent than any sexual technique or position, is the power of an encouraging word aptly spoken. When you feel tender toward your spouse, say it. Say something! It may not come out all suave and smooth, but God will mix in His creativity, and you might just surprise yourself with what you hear coming out of your mouth.

We discovered the power of encouraging words while on our honeymoon. I (Pam) had just stepped from the shower and was looking in the mirror. I began to criticize my body. Bill was sitting on the bed, admiring his new wife. As I would comment on an area I thought needed improving, Bill began to panic. He was afraid I would continue to point out my shortcomings and then get depressed and sex would be out of the question. I went on for a few minutes until he could stand it no longer. He was angry that I would put down his choice of a wife. I was not only tearing down myself, but undermining Bill's taste as well. Instead of saying something in anger, he prayed, "God, I could do a better job than that mirror!"

He stood up, wrapped his arms around me, and told me to look straight into his eyes. He very seriously and very lovingly said, "I will be your mirror. My eyes will reflect your beauty. You are beautiful, Pamela. You are perfect, and if you ever doubt it, come stand before me. The mirror of my eyes will tell you the true story. You are perfect for me. If I have to throw away every mirror in the house to get you to believe me, I will! From now on, let me be your mirror."

For more than 25 years, Bill has reflected to me my worth and value from God's point of view. A man does himself a favor by loving his wife and being her mirror because she will want to love him the way he desires to be loved.

For our twenty-fifth wedding anniversary, our friends Boomer and Lisa wrote a song that carries the message of the mirror. Each day, when your spouse looks at you as he or she rolls over in bed to face you, leans up to kiss you, or turns to talk to you, tell yourself, "I will be your mirror."

I Will Be Your Mirror

Words and Music by Boomer & Lisa Reiff

VERSE

She looked into the mirror on that sacred night
Hoping her reflection had somehow changed
The image looking back at her wasn't what she wanted to see
Mirror, mirror on the wall…

VERSE

As he watched her from a distance he could read her mind
He knew the way she felt and how her heart cried out
And he wondered at this lovely girl—how she could be so blind
'Cause when he looked at her the only thing he saw was beautiful…

CHORUS

I will be your mirror
Reflecting the beauty of your face
You are lovely and gentle
A picture of God's amazing grace
I will see in you what you can't see in yourself
And I will tell you again and again
I will be your mirror

VERSE

She turned back from the mirror and felt her heart sink low
As she told him all the things she'd like to change
Her smile, her eyes, her nose, her skin—she would change them
   if she could
How many times she'd prayed that she could just feel beautiful…
So he took her face into his hands as he spoke the words so true
Look to me for your reflection and I promise you, I promise you…

CHORUS

BRIDGE

And now she looks back on her life
At all the years that have come and gone
And she knows the gift he gave that day

Became the ground she's walked upon
When he said,

CHORUS
I will be your mirror...

Hands-on Homework

At your wedding, there may have been a song you chose that carried your heart, or perhaps you danced to an "our song." Put on the same song and dance in your bedroom, with or without clothing, and whisper the words of the song into your spouse's ear. Play it again while you make love. Remember all the moments you have loved each other. Whisper recollections of your red-hot monogamy moments as you dance, hold each other, and make love. Remembering rekindles the romance and reignites the red-hot monogamy God intended for you two to share.

Red-Hot
ROMANCE IDEAS

176. On your mate's half birthday, create a private "all about you" day or 24 hours away. Do his or her special activities, eat delicious food, and enjoy his or her favorite intimate acts for one 24-hour period.

177. Opposites attract. For one day, flip roles. If he usually drives, then let her. If she usually cooks, let him. If he's usually on top, have her do the honors.

178. Love long-distance: We both travel quite a bit, and we minister often to military couples that are separated for months at a time. Here's a few ways to stay in love over the miles:

- Read the same marriage book and e-mail or talk by phone about what you are learning.
- Sleep in his shirt.
- Send him a little piece of something lacy you usually wear. (Cutting a corner off the hem and sliding it into a love note will do.)
- Tuck love notes in his or her suitcase.
- Wrap small gifts and number them so that they can open one per day on their trip, or hide them in his or her work items (files, briefcase, cell phone case).
- Get a picture frame that has a message recorder and record a love message for him or her.
- Put favorite pictures on a slide show on their laptop.

- Send cards to the hotels they are planning to stay at (or other small gifts).

- Leave voice mails when you know they can't be reached (while on a plane or in a meeting).

- Send comfort from home: their favorite slippers, treats from the local candy store, pictures of the kids.

- Create a pocket pinup calendar. Add snapshots into the pages of a small pocket-sized organizer. (Don't put in any pictures you wouldn't mind having someone else get ahold of just in case it gets lost.)

- Write one long continuous love letter and send it back and forth. Just change the color of pen (or over e-mail change font color with every new addition). Then, when you get lonely, all that great lovin' is in one place for you to read!

- Tape phone calls so if the time zone (or the war zone) keeps calls far apart, you can at least replay the ones you have to hear his or her voice.

179. **Prom for adults.** Rent a limo and attend a charity ball. Or simply rent a limo for the four-hour minimum and drive around eating caviar and drinking your favorite beverage. Most limos have a privacy window that rolls up for a reason.

180. **Take a break in the action.** On one of those very long trips, plan a layover in a city for sightseeing, or rent a hotel room for six hours in the afternoon and take a Jacuzzi and a "nap" before catching the plane.

181. **Come rescue me!** When the one you love is under a rugged deadline, bring the party to him or her. Pack a few

things to relax your mate: favorite foods, some soothing music, and then go give your mate a massage.

182. If you are the boss, have sex in your office (after hours to ensure privacy). If you don't have a sofa, the desk will do—and you'll never look at work quite the same way. (For an extra thrill, in the back of a drawer, leave a surprise "memento" from the night.)

183. Play the "You are better than…" game. See who can one up with the best compliment. "You are better than wine." "You are better than chocolate." "You are better than the fireworks at Disneyland." "You are better than Christmas morning."

184. Hire a quartet to come sing old-fashioned love songs to your spouse while on a date or when he or she is at the office. ("Let me call you sweetheart…")

185. Have a formal vow renewal ceremony. Invite family and friends, or just have the two of you and a pastor.

186. Have a tickle fight, a pillow fight, or wrestling match.

187. Go all day without saying anything negative, without giving an "I told you so" look, or "suggesting" what he or she should do.

188. Go to the mall. Each of you are given the same amount of money and time to buy a complete outfit for one another.

189. Try having a "yes, dear" attitude all day (you don't have to say it; just choose to give your spouse's opinion the green light all day with no arguments or debate).

190. Learn to understand something your mate loves (the rules of football, how to golf, fly fishing, how to find a great antique or quilt).

191. Go on a date where you do something nice for someone else. Drop off groceries at a newlywed's apartment, flowers on the doorstep of someone who is shut in, work at a homeless shelter. You will realize your love can be a strength for others to lean on.

192. Kiss your mate in public the way you kiss him or her in private. Kiss the entire way up or down in the elevator of a high-rise. Kiss at every stoplight.

193. Forgive. And give a gift that lets your spouse know you have forgiven. (For more on this see our book *Love, Honor and Forgive*.)

194. Place romantic cards throughout the house or use the house for some play on words. One Christmas Bill woke up to signs that read, "You are my CUP of tea." "I love to STAIR at you!" "You've opened the DOOR to my heart."

195. Play a twist on compliments and banter back and forth an "I'm glad you don't…" game. For example: "I'm glad you don't belch (at least very often)." "I'm glad you don't nag." "I'm glad you don't order me around."

196. Place your teddies inside his suit jackets, and see the smile before he heads out the door for a business meeting.

197. Write a mini romance novel where you two are the main characters.

198. Every time you pass the keys, the salt, or some other item, say "I love you" and kiss.

199. Rent a bicycle built for two or a paddleboat and test how well you can work together outside the bedroom!

200. Buy a bearskin rug—or put in a fireplace. Add something to your room that says "Red-hot monogamy is a priority!"

NOTES

Chapter 1—Sex! What Makes It Red-Hot?

1. Bill and Pam Farrel, *Single Men Are Like Waffles—Single Women Are Like Spaghetti* (Eugene, OR: Harvest House Publishers, 2002), p. 165.

2. www.collegesexperts.blogspot.com

3. www.healthwisemag.com/archive/2002/HWfeatwin02b.htm

4. www.gymamerica.com/gti/magazine/magazine_qa/0,3291,1_cid_729,00.html

Chapter 2—Bringing the Honeymoon Home

1. Pam Farrel, *The 10 Best Decisions a Woman Can Make* (Eugene, OR: Harvest House Publishers, 2004), p. 113.

2. Dave and Claudia Arp, *No Time for Sex* (West Monroe, LA: Howard Publishing Company, 2004), p. 47.

3. Clifford and Joyce Penner, *The Gift of Sex* (Nashville, TN: W Publishing Group, 2003), p. 197.

4. Cathy Horning, message delivered to MOPS 2/2005. Cathy is a speaker and may be contacted at cehorning@sbcglobal.net.

5. Arp, *No Time for Sex*, p. 89.

Chapter 3—The Great Escape, Part 1

1. www.freerepublic.com/focus/f-news/937134/posts

2. www.my.webmd.com/content/article/91/100941.htm?z=1687_00000_0000_fi_03

3. news.bbc.co.uk/1/hi/magazine/3555734.stm

4. Ibid.

5. www.sextherapyny.com/fitness.htm

6. www.bodybuildingforyou.com/articles-submit/ghf/better-sex-1.htm

Chapter 4—The Great Escape, Part 2

1. Tim and Beverly LaHaye, *The Act of Marriage After 40* (Grand Rapids, MI: Zondervan, 2000), p. 35.

2. Adapted from *When Perfect Isn't Enough,* Copyright © 2003 by Nancy Kennedy. Used by permission of WaterBrook Press, Colorado Springs, CO. All rights reserved.

Chapter 5—Come on, Baby, Light My Fire, Part 1

1. LaHaye, *The Act of Marriage After 40,* p. 85.

2. "Passionate Intimacy" from the *Life Enrich* video, featuring Dog Rosenau, Chris McClusky, Michael Sytsma, and Debra Taylor (American Association of Christian Counselors: Lynchurg, VA); www.aacc.net

3. Excerpted from Jill Savage, "Schedule Sex?" *Marriage Partnership,* Summer 2005, pp. 20-22. Used by permission.

4. Shared in a conversation with Pam Farrel.

Chapter 7—Sizzling Sex

1. Clifford and Joyce Penner, *The Gift of Sex* (Nashville, TN: W Publishing Group, 2003), p. 208.

Chapter 8—Browsing in the Wonder of Each Other

1. www.healthnnutrition.co.in/display_Standard.asp?section=sex&subsection=features&xml=January2004_features_standard7

2. Penner, *The Gift of Sex,* p. 214.

To contact Bill and Pam Farrel:

Farrel Communications
Masterful Living
P.O. Box 1507
San Marcos, CA 92079

800-810-4449

www.farrelcommunications.com

OTHER BOOKS BY
BILL AND PAM FARREL

Men Are Like Waffles—
Women Are Like Spaghetti

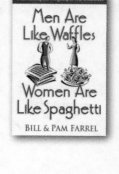

Bill and Pam Farrel explain why a man is like a waffle (each element of his life is in a separate box), why a woman is like spaghetti (everything in her life touches everything else), and what these differences mean. Then they show readers how to achieve more satisfying relationships.

Biblical insights, sound research, humorous anecdotes, and real-life stories make this guide entertaining and practical. Readers will feast on enticing insights that include:

- letting gender differences work for them
- achieving fulfillment in romantic relationships
- coordinating parenting so kids receive good, consistent care

Much of the material in this rewarding book will also improve interactions with family, friends, and coworkers.

Why Men and Women
Act the Way They Do

Building on the popularity of their "Waffles and Spaghetti" books, the Farrels combine humor with solid research in a book designed to help men and women move past conflicts caused by innate sexual differences.

Those who want to understand the opposite sex will find a gold mine of information in *Why Men and Women Act the Way They Do*, including:

- Are there differences in the genders at birth?
- How do differences in the way a child is raised affect adult relationships?
- What do men and women love to talk about...and why?

Every Marriage Is
a Fixer-Upper

Bestselling authors and popular speakers Bill and Pam Farrel provide readers with a tool chest of communication skills for do-it-yourselfers who want to get the most out of their marriage. HGTV watchers and *Better Homes and Gardens* readers will quickly connect with the home-improvement theme as the Farrels show couples how to...

- strengthen the foundation of their family
- inspect their marriage for hidden weak spots
- protect their relational investment with consistent maintenance and improvement

Filled with practical advice, biblical insights, and the Farrels' trademark warmth and wit, this manual is perfect for newlyweds as well as longtime marriage partners as they turn their fixer-upper marriage into the relationship of their dreams.